Speech, Silence, Action!

JOURNEYS IN FAITH

Creative Dislocation—The Movement of Grace
Robert McAfee Brown

Hope Is an Open Door
Mary Luke Tobin

By Way of Response
Martin E. Marty

Speech, Silence, Action!
The Cycle of Faith

Virginia Ramey Mollenkott

Journeys in Faith
Robert A. Raines, Editor

ABINGDON
Nashville

SPEECH, SILENCE, ACTION!
The Cycle of Faith

Library of Congress Cataloging in Publication Data

MOLLENKOTT, VIRGINIA R
    Speech, silence, action!
    (Journeys in faith)
    1. Christian life—1960-   2.   Mollenkott, Virginia R.   3.   Chris-
tian biography—United States   I.   Title.   II.   Series.
            BV4501.2.M554   248.4   80-15812

ISBN 0-687-39169-5

Scripture quotations unless otherwise noted are from the Revised Standard
Version of the Bible, copyrighted 1946, 1952, © 1971, 1973 by the Division of
Christian Education of the National Council of the Churches of Christ in the
U.S.A. and used by permission.

Scripture quotations noted NEB are from The New English Bible. © the
Delegates of the Oxford University Press and the Syndics of the Cambridge
University Press 1961, 1970. Reprinted by permission.

Quotation on page 97 is from *EveryOne: The Timeless Myth of "Everyman" Reborn*
by Frederick Franck. Copyright © 1978 by Frederick Franck. Published by
Doubleday. Used by permission of author.

MANUFACTURED BY THE PARTHENON PRESS AT
NASHVILLE, TENNESSEE, UNITED STATES OF AMERICA

This book is lovingly dedicated to

Lynne E. Pattin
Letha and John Scanzoni
Beverly Cofrancesco
Ralph Blair
Catherine Barry
Janet Leonard
Robert and Cindy Raines
Marion S. Lill
my son, Paul F. Mollenkott

and others who have shown generous
interest in my work
and who know all about me
and love me just the same

Contents

Editor's Foreword

People inside and outside the church today are engaged in a profound revisioning of the faith journey. Wanting to honor our own heritage and to be nourished by our roots, we also want to discern the signs of the kingdom now, and to move into the 1980s with a lean, biblical, ecumenical, and human faith perspective.

The *Journeys in Faith* book series is offered to facilitate this revisioning of faith. Reflecting on the social justice openings of the 1960s and the inward searching of the 1970s, these books articulate a fresh integration of the faith journey for the years ahead. They are personal and social. Authors have been invited to share what has been happening to them in their faith and life in recent years, and then to focus on issues that have become primary for them in this time.

We believe that these lucidly written books will be widely used by study groups in congregations, seminaries, colleges, renewal centers, orders, and denominations, as well as by individuals for personal study and reflection.

Our authors embody a diversity of experience and perspective, which will provide many points of identification and enrichment for readers. As we enter into the pilgrimages shared in these books we will find resonance, encouragement, and insight for a fresh appropriation of our faith, toward personal and social transformation.

Virginia Mollenkott has written a "bridge" which will

provide a meeting ground for liberals and conservatives, evangelicals and activists. Her story begins in a fundamentalist setting where, overweight and lonely, she experienced a "humiliating childhood." Her reading and life experience taught her to learn from dreams, classic literature, and mystics, feminists, and always, the Bible. She describes her journey from biblicism to seeing social justice as a "central sign of the Holy Spirit." She allows us to share her struggle out of a judgmental spirit toward a spirit of magnanimity. Readers will be moved by her passion and compassion.

She centers on biblical feminism as a central issue in the life of church and society and in her own life. Touching on language and imagery about God, obesity, the polarity of art and technology, homosexuality, sexism, body-spirit unity, she articulates a biblically based "mutuality" in social relationships. Readers will appreciate her rich knowledge of literature as well as her involvement in action groups. She writes with evangelical fervor and hope. She is at once analytical and imaginative, deeply convinced, persuasive. She has found a balanced integrity with which many readers will want to identify.

This book will be especially useful for persons seeking to understand one another and to draw together for mutual witness and dialogue. It is a reconciling book that will enable readers to get in touch with the dynamics of their own faith journey and with that of others. It will be useful for councils of churches, denominations, and local congregations seeking study material for growth in understanding and cooperation. Hers is a book that gives us hope for a gathering of evangelicals and activists committed to rebuilding the church today.

Robert A. Raines

Speech, Silence, Action!

Get ready, get set, *go!* How many childhood games begin with that rhythmic chant! If there seems to be an analogy to my title, be assured that the similarity is not coincidence.

My development during approximately the past fifteen years has, in one sense, been a development away from an almost entire focus on words, book, and ideas (speech), through a time of learning about silence, and finally into the field of action. It could be charted this way:

SPEECH → SILENCE → ACTION

But in another, deeper sense, what has developed is a life-style in which speech, silence, and action form a constantly renewed cycle, so that the chart would look more like this:

Even my interior life is structured according to this dynamic. I continue whenever possible to feed my spirit with great words from the past and present—the Bible, Christian and non-Christian mystics, classical literature, contemporary literature. So the word remains very central as a stimulant and preparer, the *get ready* stage of my life-experiences. Then, when I begin to pray, for the first few minutes speech continues in the foreground. Aloud or silently, I speak and feel my concerns for others and myself. But even more important to me are the moments when the words recede, and in the silence I contemplate the One Being, the Fountainhead of my being and every being, the Light invisible to every eye except the inner one. Sometimes during those moments, realizations come to me about people I should contact, attitudes I should work to change, growth I need to make, things I need to do. Sometimes, on the back of my eyelids, I see energy pulsing toward me. But mostly, the peace, the love, the silence. This is my *get set* stage, the most delicate, difficult to protect, and valuable time of every day. Without it, burnout is inevitable. After it, I am ready to go into action.

I remember, just about fifteen years ago, asking a well-known missionary to define for me what she was positively, absolutely certain about (today we might call it "the bottom line"). She thought for only a few seconds before replying, "I am certain that there is a God—and

that God loves me." I remember standing rooted to the
kitchen floor in awe and misery. Misery because I was
envious. I shared no such certainty. My inner experience
at that time was far better characterized by these words
from a sonnet by Gerard Manley Hopkins:

> O the mind, mind has mountains; cliffs of fall
> Frightful, sheer, no-man-fathomed. Hold them cheap
> May who ne'er hung there.

I was not one of the people who could hold cheap the
dizzying cliffs, the sheer drop-offs of doubt and horror
within the human mind. For I had "hung there,"
looking fearfully downward into interior possibilities
that frightened me.

What has made the difference in me? I am tempted to
say that meditation, the silence, the *get set* stage, is what
has made all the difference. But that would be only
partially true. Some of my inner transformation has
stemmed from a change in the *get ready* stage—more
daring reading patterns, a willingness to open myself to
speech that formerly I feared exposure to—especially
the social activist and mystical writings I had been taught
to mistrust as too heretical. And some of it has come from
plunging into action, putting myself out there on the line
for causes that seemed authentically my vocation. (I am
reminded of John 7:17, where Jesus comments that
those who *do* God's will will *know* the doctrine.) Certainty
comes not from waiting till all the facts are in—all the
facts will never be in during anyone's limited human
experience—but rather from acting as authentically as
possible, trying to keep sensitively attuned to the pitch
pipe of the inner ear.

Still, at the center of it all is the silence. As Robert Frost
loved to say,

We dance round in a ring and suppose,
But the Secret sits in the middle and knows.

Too much dancing in the ring is too much *go*, too much activism. (One of the greatest dangers faced by all the social activists I know is taking ourselves so seriously that we cannot turn any opportunity down, as if single-handedly we had to save the world, with the result that sometimes we stagger from loss of center.) Too much supposing is too much cognition, too many words, too much theorizing, too much speech. (We who care about the gospel on both the personal and societal levels can easily become overwhelmed with the details of trying to understand *how* to wrestle with the principalities and powers.) When that happens, we inevitably lose the source of our power. The result is paralysis. The only way to engage in a spiritual warfare without losing a peaceful, joyful heart is to maintain constantly renewed contact with "the Secret [who] sits in the middle and knows."

A group of black evangelical musicians known as Andraé Crouch and the Disciples do a song that expresses what I'm trying to say about the all-important *get set* period:

It's those quiet times, quiet times
They put that sparkle back in my eyes . . .
That's when I tell You that I love You,
And You remind me that You love me too,
Together there is nothing we can't do.
No, they can't take them away from me,
Oh, no, they can't take them away from
me.*

"They can't take them away from me"; the words bring to my mind the fear I used to have that some day, because of my beliefs or whatever, I might be put into solitary confinement and cut off from everybody I love. Occasionally, during my silences, the memory of that fear floats across my mind like a nearly forgotten object. And I realize that the thought no longer holds the same terror that once it held. I am certainly not eager for trouble, and it would be a colossal fake to pass myself off as a person who experiences no doubt or fear. But I have noticed that as long as I keep myself centered, my fear of abandonment diminishes almost to the vanishing point. I feel less and less troubled by nasty remarks about me in the press, or about reports of ugly gossip, or about hate letters. And as I reflect on it, the reason I no longer feel terror about solitary confinement or the isolating circumstances symbolized by that kind of punishment is precisely this: that as long as I have any consciousness at all, nobody can cut me off from access to "the Secret [who] sits in the middle and knows." *"They can't take that away from me."* Nothing whatsoever can separate me from the love of God. I may not know why certain things happen to me. I do not need to know, because the Secret at my center knows and empowers my being.

So it is because I have been graciously guided into a dynamic cycle of speech, silence, and action that I no longer feel misery at other people's certainty that there is a God who loves them. I share that certainty. And I want to share that Good News with those who are not yet in touch with it. The world is full of people whose lives have been so oppressed by grinding injustice that it might seem a mockery to them to be told that there is a God who loves them. Speech alone is not a sufficient response to their need. They need the empowerment to find their *own* contact with the Secret at the center. So out of the silence springs—*must* spring—action. I cannot honestly pray "thy will be done" in the silent times without carrying forward that prayer into attempts to bring about that will on earth.

Part of my renaissance of faith during the past few years has been the increasing conviction that the will of God is the creation of a New Humanity, a New World, a reign of Christ's peace and justice through mutuality on a global scale. This conviction has grown through renewed study of Scripture invigorated by new patterns of reading, new people I have met, and new insights recorded on the back of my eyelids.

But I have run ahead of myself. Let's begin at the beginning of the particular story I want to tell you, starting with the most cognitive, propositional era of my life.

PART ONE: SPEECH

1
Survival Time

Fifteen years ago I was just completing my Ph.D. in English Literature at New York University. I remember the health-wrecking tension of those Ph.D. years: teaching full time and chairing the English Department at Shelton College, taking care of a small son and being responsible for the washing, ironing, bed-making, cleaning, shopping, cooking—the works. I remember feeling it was unfair that my husband could get up from dinner and watch TV all evening while I washed the dishes, put the baby to bed, and then cleared a place for myself on the kitchen table to study for my graduate courses and prepare for my next day's classes. I frequently worked until the wee hours, always struggling to shut out the sound of the incessant television.

One semester, I remember, I carried three graduate courses on one evening, and at the end of the semester, after a day of teaching, had to write one two-hour final exam, then another, and then a third. I did it that way because I could afford neither the time nor the money to drive to New York several times a week. I made a game of it all, telling myself that I did not have to get the Ph.D. all at once, just one requirement at a time. I thought of each requirement as a hurdle I was jumping: the preliminary exam, the ten courses one by one, the French exam, the German exam, the oral exam, the doctoral dissertation. Just one thing at a time. And I vowed to myself that I would never ask for any special consideration because of the heavy burden I was carrying—no extension of course paper deadlines, no extra help, no excuse from any assignment.

Meanwhile, I followed a rigid policy of returning all my own students' papers from the five separate courses I was teaching, graded and with comments, within one week of the time I received them so that the students would not have time to lose interest in their results. I remember reports that when one of my colleagues heard about my policy, he told his students that I was compulsive. Perhaps that was true. But maybe a kinder approach would have been to say that I was trying to survive. Because there was never any letup, summer or winter, to let myself fall behind would have been fatal.

When the Ph.D. was completed, I faced other pressures that I had been postponing. Like the fact that my marriage was hopeless. Like the fact that I was extremely lonely and starved for emotional support. Like the fact that my health was poor. (Adrenal exhaustion, the doctor said, and it left me susceptible to infections, perpetually tired, frequently dizzy.) By this time I had left Shelton College and was teaching at Nyack Missionary College. I was just beginning to catch a glimpse of a broader Christian universe than my fundamentalist upbringing had led me to anticipate. In 1967, suspecting that some day I might have to get a divorce and sensing that the job market might tighten, I left Nyack for the state college where I still teach.

Why am I recounting all this? As a way of explaining, I think, why I came to understand the social justice implications of the gospel so very late in my life. I have been grieved by the fact that I did not take a stand against the Vietnam War until close to the end of it. When someone mentioned that fact in a letter published by *The Other Side*, I felt overwhelmed with shame. But when I think about the years I spent at Shelton College, where I had gone fresh from my M.A. to give my husband a chance to complete college and a Master's Degree, and when I remember that during all those years I was fed with Carl McIntire's theories of communist conspiracy and the horrors of liberal Christianity, I feel less embarrassed by my slow evolution. Both during my undergraduate years at Bob Jones University and during nine years at Shelton, even Billy Graham was continually attacked as too liberal. I was warned against the spiritual dangers of reading someone as liberal as C. S. Lewis. "Liberal" was a dirty word at Shelton, and I trembled when an angry student applied it to me. By contrast, the Nyack atmosphere of the Christian and Missionary Alliance seemed like a wide-open field of freedom.

Still, there was the atmosphere at home, where my husband assured me that all troubles in our marriage were the result of my own childishness. Mature women, particularly if they believed God's Word, had no difficulty with their subordinate role in church and home. My gradually opening vision seemed to Fred very threatening, very wrong, very heretical. The day that the students were shot at Kent State University may serve as a good capsule summary of what life was like in our home. Having spent so much of my life with college-aged young people, I felt as if some of my own children had been assassinated, and I wept. Fred regarded my tears with disgust. "Crying shows that you don't believe the Bible," he said. "Why so?" I sniffled. "Because the Bible says the magistrate bears not the sword in vain. Those guards were only doing what God expects magistrates to do, preserve law and order!" I made no reply because experience had taught me replies were useless.

Those were survival years, and I survived. I vaguely remember reading to my son a passage from a George MacDonald fairy tale about climbing a hill and meeting a person resting about halfway up. MacDonald suggested that on the hill of morality, one should always reserve judgment until one has discovered whether the person who is resting has been *on the way down* or *on the way up*. So for those of you who wonder where I was during the worst of the 1960s when you needed all the help you could get, the answer is that I was sorting through my fundamentalist heritage and otherwise very busy just surviving. But according to my own light and to the limits of my strength, I was attempting to climb.

2
The Bible as Both Normative and Emancipating

It is difficult for people who have not known a fundamentalist background to believe the basic, almost primitive struggles such a background can generate in fundamentalist persons as they become educated. What I deeply appreciate from my own background is that I was thoroughly grounded in the surface facts (the words themselves) of the Bible. For that I feel grateful to my mother and to various brothers at the Plymouth Brethren Assemblies. I specify the *brothers*, of course, because if any of the sisters knew anything much about the Bible, I had no way of being aware of their knowledge. Women were not permitted to preach, or to pray aloud, or even to ask questions at the Bible "readings" (interpretative sessions). However, no one ever tried to say that women should not study the Bible for their own enlightenment, and my strenuous efforts at

Scripture memorization were regarded with amused tolerance. But as far as real Scripture *scholarship* about the canon, the texts, the historical milieu, and so forth, I never encountered it until I was working on my doctoral dissertation on *Milton and the Apocrypha*. I stood in the New York Public Library, amazed and awed by an entire *wall* of card catalogue drawers devoted to works of biblical scholarship.

In my own youthful milieu, it had been a daring act to read any biblical version other than the King James. For a Plymouth Brethren believer, it was even a daring act to accept any annotations or commentaries that differed substantially from those of the Scofield Reference Bible, which dated the creation of the world at 4000 B.C. The cognitive dissonance set up in people of my background when they are confronted with modern science is in a very literal sense staggering. Enormous amounts of energy are expended simply in trying to arrive where other people assume everyone to have been from the start!

For instance, during the last fifteen years I have spent tremendous energy just trying to understand whether my deepest being is wholly evil or whether I might dare to believe that God is truly present in my deepest self. Back in 1966 when I was writing my first book, *Adamant and Stone-Chips: A Christian Humanist Approach to Knowledge*, I felt very daring to assert that even "unsaved" human beings have valid gifts, and that even modern literature with its relativism and subjectivism has something important to say to the Christian faith. I had been reading people such as Harvey Cox and H. Richard Niebuhr, but I never would have had the nerve to believe what they told me about "secular" culture if I had not been studying great Renaissance Christian humanists like John Milton, Francis Bacon, and John Donne. Those classical Christian authors, encountered during my graduate studies, gave me the courage to look more deeply at what my liberal contemporaries were saying about the human role in the divine plan. I made a practice of testing what I read in them against what the Bible had to say about human intellect and artistry.

In his essay "Of Education," John Milton had written that young people should be taught the Greek and Roman classics (the backbone of Renaissance humanism) with the important qualification that every day, everything they had learned should be subjected to the "determinate sentence" of the ethical and doctrinal teachings of the Bible. To this very day, that is my method. To the limits of my time and strength, I try to be open to the insights of my contemporaries, because those insights cast a whole new light on both the literary tradition and the Scriptures. Sociology, psychology, anthropology, history, you name it: all of these disciplines teach me new questions to ask and therefore cause new light to break forth from the Word of God. But I adhere firmly to the practice of subjecting everything that I learn to what for me will always be the "determinate sentence" of Scripture.

I realize, of course, that my dogged loyalty to the Bible is regarded by some of my friends and readers with either irritation or amusement. The more psychologically attuned explain it as my inability to make a complete break from the teachings of my youth. Their explanation in no way threatens me, even as I feel unthreatened by attempts to explain prayer away as "nothing but" autosuggestion. I have very little time for "nothing but," *either/or* kinds of thinking. To me, for instance, a scientific explanation of how a baby is born only enhances rather than diminishes the sheer wonder of the reproductive process. So without worrying about how others may label me, I continue to regard the Bible as given by God for my doctrine, reproof, correction, and instruction in righteousness.

The irony is that I am regarded as a flaming radical in some of the very same circles that would agree most with my submission of myself to the biblical norm. My belief that the Bible teaches the *mutual* concern, service, and subjection of husband and wife is still considered heretical in many of those circles. And my views regarding homosexuality are utter anathema! After many years of thinking otherwise and after much study, I have learned that the Bible is silent about the homosexual orientation and about homosexual love (as opposed to exploitative sexual *acts*) and therefore leaves the Christian free to respond humanely to homosexual persons in the light of modern scientific understandings. That belief has branded me as radical even in some of the "post-liberal" circles that used to seem in my youth so far to my left that they were not even Christian.

At the moment it seems that I may be destined to be forever marginal: too "radical" for most evangelicals, too "addicted to the Bible" for many people in the main-line churches. (The big difference is that whereas some fundamentalist-evangelicals have repudiated my person and my beliefs with real venom, many people from main-line Protestantism, Roman Catholicism, Judaism, and transreligious groups have treated me with respect and even tenderness. It's an important distinction, one worth pondering.) I would like my own attitudes to remain loving toward people across the whole spectrum because I think we need one another.

Difficult as it may be for my fundamentalist family and

friends to realize, it is precisely my study of the Bible that has radicalized me. While I in no way wish to minimize the importance of the insights I have gained from reading the works of biblical scholars and theologians past and present, or works in various other scholarly disciplines, I have resisted any insights that I was unable to square with my understanding of the Bible after I had circled round and round its texts armed with my new questions and new angles of vision. I realize, of course, that this stance still leaves me vulnerable to charges that I have blinded myself to certain insights, or conversely that I have been too ingenious in accommodating my understanding of the Bible to modern points of view. There is no way anyone can be certain enough to defend herself or himself from such charges. Indeed, to be *too* certain is to be idolatrous.

What I *can* say is that never have I consciously taken a position in defiance of or unconcern about biblical teachings. And I subscribe to the idea that no Christian person should be charged with heresy who has tried to be faithful to the Word of God after conscientious study of it. I picked up that attitude from another Milton essay, "Of True Religion, Heresy, Schism, Toleration"; and Milton knew what he was talking about because he had frequently been considered heretical for his views on divorce, and had more than once committed acts of civil disobedience that could well have put his neck under the hatchet. As Milton himself put it, "Heresy is the will and choice professedly against scripture; error is . . . misunderstanding the scripture after all serious endeavors to understand it rightly. . . . 'Err I may, but a heretic I will not be.' "

Turning from right to left, I should like to suggest to my more liberal-minded friends that it might be worthwhile, even from a hard-nosed strategical point of view, to consider the implications of the fact that it is my study of Scripture that has led me to an ecumenical and universalist vision. Remember, now, that I speak as a person who thought at first that the only people in heaven would be the Plymouth Brethren, with a few exceptions from among the more fundamentalist of the churches. I distinctly remember eyeing The United Methodist Church with disdain, because people sometimes smoked on the front steps. (Now I feel very comfortable with Methodists and experience a sense of solidarity with them.) I wondered what kind of horrors went on inside a nearby Protestant Episcopal Church, which to my biased eyes resembled a prison. (Now I know what goes on, since I am Episcopalian.) My friends and I crossed the street to avoid being on the sidewalk next to the Roman Catholic Church; to us, Catholics were a disease. I remember the slight jolt I felt when first I realized that Catholics considered themselves Christians. (Now, of course, I consider it an honor to participate in Catholic liturgy whenever the opportunity arises.)

I think my own experience suggests that teaching the Bible from a liberating perspective is an excellent tool for ecumenists to use in the attempt to stimulate in people an all-inclusive, global vision of human justice, dignity, and oneness. I realize that very few people at the grass roots actually sit down and read the Bible, let alone study it seriously. Nevertheless, most people feel respect for the Bible and do not want to defy its teachings. It is precisely the combination of respectful awe and lack of firsthand knowledge that renders people so gullible toward far-right leaders like Phyllis Schlafly (anti-ERA), Anita Bryant (anti-gay), Marabel Morgan *(The Total Woman),* or Bill Gothard (Basic Youth Conflicts Seminars, which

teach thousands that women should relate to God
indirectly, through male authority-figures). The only
way to provide protection from manipulation by those
who claim to have the infallible inside track on God's
exclusion of certain people from first-class personhood is
to teach people the basics of the Bible from a more
liberating perspective.

The case for an all-inclusive, egalitarian, nondualistic,
global Body of Christ—the single organism of the New
Humanity—can be made from numerous passages in the
Bible. It is of course important to avoid the "supermarket
approach" of proof-texting from a single remark
wrenched out of its context and possibly faulty in its
English translation. We have had enough of that in sexist
plucking out of context such passages as Ephesians 5:22
(wifely submission) or I Timothy 2:12: "I suffer not a
woman to teach" (KJV). If the case for organic unity is to
be honest as well as convincing, we need to make it from a
holistic reading of the Bible, which not only places each
passage against its primary historical context but also
allows other Scriptures to provide commentary on its
meaning.

Following such principles, it is not difficult to make a
case for ecumenism from Ephesians 3 (to which I will
return later). Or from Galatians 3, especially the
wonderful image of putting on Christ like a garment that
encases and covers and eradicates all our racial, sexual,
and classist-economic barriers. Or from Isaiah 11:1-10,
concerning the peaceful and righteous reign of the
Branch of Jesse. The case for global unity can also be
made from Romans 12 or I Corinthians 12 or Colossians
1:15-20; or from the vision of I John 3, that love of
humanity *is* love of God. Or from Acts 17 with its great
womb-image of a God in whom all nations live and move

and have their being. Or from the words in Matthew 25 of the King concerning his siblings (not just *brothers*, incidentally; the word used here, usually translated *brothers*, is *adelphoi*, which means "from the same womb"). The possibilities go on and on.

In these days of a grass-roots evangelical/fundamentalist revival, it is vitally important for ecumenists to bear in mind that for most of these people, social justice seems like an unbiblical, secular concept. To them, salvation is a private matter and ethics and morality are private matters. For many of them there is no hope for societal structures until after the Second Coming of Christ (interpreted literally as an appearance in the sky). They need to hear the Good News that the Bible's frequent words about righteousness refer to *justice*. They need to hear that God's love is unconditional and universal, not just in the sense of offering personal salvation to those who will listen, but in the sense of filling the whole earth with the knowledge of the Lord as the waters cover the sea (Isa. 11:9). My experience suggests that it is the militant teaching of these *biblical* ecumenical insights, and only that teaching, which stands a chance of convicting, convincing, and mobilizing the millions of evangelicals in the United States. It's worth a try. The alternative may well be some form of neofascism—an ultra-authoritarian form of rationalism.

Since my activity in the biblical feminist (human equality) movement, the views of the Evangelical Women's Caucus, which I share, have been attacked chiefly from two quarters: by those who think that feminism contradicts the Bible and that feminism must go, and by those who *agree* that feminism contradicts the Bible but think that the Bible must go. It is a shock to realize that the farthest *right* and the farthest *left*-wing elements in contemporary society are in full agreement that the Bible and human justice are antithetical. No wonder the ERA has still not been ratified! No wonder people in the huge central group of society (neither radical right nor left) are confused! No wonder they are easy prey to manipulation by those who offer a simplistic and repressive reading of the Bible! Most people, whether in organized religion or outside of it, do not want to defy the God of the Bible and yet do not want to be inhumane or unjust to other human beings. The way to build bridges and foster healing and faith is to show such people that when contextually interpreted, the Bible is not repressive but liberating. Thus, their instincts toward simple fairness do not pit them against the Bible, but align them with it.

3
The Liberating Arts

Anyone who has taught at the high school or college level can testify, as I can, that anti-intellectualism and/or anti-humanism is a strong strain in the United States, particularly in Protestantism. And the more conservative the political and religious stance, the more anti-intellectual other attitudes tend to become (although of course there are some brilliant exceptions). The most extreme example of obscurantism would be the Bible Belt preacher who prayed fervently, "Lord, make me ignorant; make me ignoranter than a mule"—on the assumption, naturally, that the greater the ignorance, the greater the faith. I remember being taught that one's attitudes toward God and humanity are analogous to a seesaw: the more you honor God, the more you debase humanity (emphasizing human depravity); and the more you exalt humanity (even in religious humanism) the more you dishonor God.

Another form taken by the human-knowledge-versus-faith dichotomy is the Jesus People Movement, which convinced many young persons that they ought to quit college because the only book they ever needed to know was the Bible (as interpreted, naturally, by the Jesus People). But the faith-knowledge conflict also resurfaces periodically among mainstream adult Christians, and is never hidden very far below the surface. A contemporary instance would be those who identify the nuclear family with God's revealed will and fear any fragmentation of that institution, refusing to believe the research of qualified sociologists and historians of the family that although the family is in transition, it is not an endangered species.

What surfaces in religious circles as a conflict between faith and knowledge, God and humanism, surfaces elsewhere as a conflict between emotionalism and rationality. I have come to believe that the roots of the deadly split between "head" and "heart" lie in sexism, which for centuries has encouraged women to be all emotion (through expressive socialization) and men to be all reason (through instrumental socialization). Because the male has been more highly valued, education has until recently focused almost entirely on the "head" (cognition, facts, reason, getting things done); but because we are all human beings with emotional natures, the devalued emotions have struck back in negative ways, such as widespread superstition and various "cults of feeling." Worship of the intellect has led to deep-seated, demoralizing distrust of it. While I was teaching in fundamentalist or evangelical colleges (until 1967), through discussion of great literature I tried to demonstrate the difference between mere emotionalism (pietistic or otherwise) and genuine emotion (always closely integrated with rational thought and clear perception). Now, at a state college, I still consider it important to give training in warmhearted thinking (or clear-minded feeling).

Just as the "war of the sexes" will end only through mutuality in the equal partnership and co-humanity of male and female, psychological wholeness comes about only through the mutuality in equal partnership of reason and emotion (including intuition).

There is no better way to foster a healthy balance between head and heart than through the study of the humanities (the liberal arts), and especially through a study of great literature (the best that has been thought and said throughout history). Unfortunately, however, because of anxiety about the shrinking job market, today's society is exalting the business major and other forms of direct job-training as superior to more theoretical studies. And in a world of nuclear reactors, genetic experiments, and computers, the study of literature has been treated like just so much fluff, fringe, or cake icing. Furthermore, some feminists wrong-headedly insist on wholesale rejection of traditional culture, including most of the religious, literary, and artistic tradition, as being so patriarchal that it is worthless. This combination of economic pressures, technological priorities, and ideological shortsightedness has been turning young people away from the very studies that (properly taught) would most enrich their experience of *being human*: theology, language, literature, history, philosophy.

Until the early 1970s when I became directly involved in issues of social justice, my only "cause" was to plead the importance of literary awareness, to defend the humanities as "the liberating arts," and to try to teach people to *read*. Very few people, I am convinced, ever learn how to read well enough; there is always the possibility of even greater sensitivity to the nuances of structure, diction, imagery, tone, point of view, and the like. My 1969 book *In Search of Balance* focused on the importance of attending to *both* poles of the many paradoxes in the Bible. Even today, a great deal of my energy still goes into trying to share reading techniques, so that people may enjoy a more holistic, liberating interpretation of the Bible. What I have done, then, is to extend myself into social justice concerns (an evangelical liberation theology) without losing any of my lifelong interest in the humanities and especially in literature.

According to my observations, contemporary discussion of the future too often centers on technological questions to the near-exclusion of concern for the quality of human interior experience. Yet as William Butler Yeats puts it, a human being is no better than a scarecrow, a "tattered coat upon a stick," unless the soul has learned to "clap its hands and sing." And apart from worship itself, the best singing school for the soul is and always has been the practice and appreciation of the arts and their systematic study in humanities courses.

Perhaps a quotation from Jane Austen's *Northanger Abbey* will make my point for me:

> "And what are you reading, Miss ——?" "Oh, it is only a novel!" replies the young lady; while she lays down her book with affected indifference, or momentary shame. —"It is only *Cecelia*, or *Camilla*, or *Belinda*"; or, in short, only some work in which . . . the most thorough knowledge of human nature, the happiest delineation of its varieties, the liveliest effusions of wit and humour are conveyed to the world in the best chosen language.

How much does twentieth-century society value a thorough knowledge of human nature? Its variety and the artistic ability to depict it accurately? Lively speech? Humor? Excellent style?

For those caught up in a crusade for human justice as crucial to Christian commitment and gospel witness, it is all too easy to fall prey to an activistic exclusivism that is yet another form of anti-intellectuality or anti-humanism. This was brought home to me recently after I had participated in a panel discussion on the subject of the Sacred and the Obscene at the Modern Language Association of America. A few weeks after the panel, I got a card from a "radical evangelical" who had been in the audience. She wrote something like this: "As I sat listening to the discussion, interesting as it was, I kept wondering what we were doing talking about such a topic in a world full of hungry and oppressed people." Immediately I felt guilty.

Why, indeed, should I have sat around discussing Mailer, Genet, Jewish mysticism, and T. S. Eliot's early poems, when there is so much work to be done in response to human need? At first my only excuse for being part of that discussion was a professional one: it is part of my job as an English teacher to concern myself with literary theory. Then came a more personal response: I was there because I thought it was where God wanted me to be at the time. Only much later—to tell the truth, right now, sitting at my typewriter—did a further realization dawn on me: I was there because discussions like that involve people in some of the deepest explorations of what it means to be human. (And it is impossible to be profoundly Christian without first being profoundly human. I heartily subscribe to the idea that "the Christian way to wash dishes is to get them clean.") I would be the first to admit that academic discussion can degenerate into egotistical oneupmanship or trivial fact-mongering; but at its best, such discussion can provide a solid basis for understanding oneself and others.

In the late 1960s, I tangled with an education professor who had written that the liberal arts tradition is totally irrelevant to modern society. His illustration of that irrelevance, drawn from Columbia University, was that Professors Highet and Hadas had been in their classrooms teaching Euripides while just outside, the Young Communist Leaguers and the social fascists had been engaged in violent quarrels. The education professor could see no value in studying Greek drama in a world of such pressing choices. My response to his argument was to stress the importance of proper method in the teaching of the humanities:

> The question is not what subject Professors Highet and Hadas were teaching: the question is how they were teaching it. If they showed the awesome parallels between Greek civilization and our own, if they taught their students to understand and emulate the magnificent thought-processes of the Greeks, if they encouraged their students to make a contribution to the human race comparable (within their own talent-potential) to the contribution made by the writers under discussion, then Professors Highet and Hadas were giving their students the best possible preparation for adequately evaluating the arguments outside the classroom walls (*NJEA Review*, Dec. 1967).

Today, nearly twelve years later, I would still make the same sort of argument for the importance of taking the time to learn (and continually reinforce) clear thinking and human *being*, especially in a world where so many are crying for assistance. Clear thought-processes are essential to the establishment of priorities, and they cannot be taught in a vacuum. Solid subject-matter is needed to provide illustration, argument, and sheer *resistance* against which the maturing mind can wrestle and strengthen its muscle. (As Cardinal Newman commented, "You can't sharpen a razor on a bar of soap.") Greek drama, when related to the contemporary scene, would provide an excellent set of timeless guidelines against which to measure timely and constantly shifting political issues.

Because of my female socialization and evangelical background, it has been with great reluctance that I have faced the fact that in a society as complex as ours, helping others on an individual basis is not enough. (It remains important, but it is not enough.) Effective action must usually be communal; individuals require institutional backing to make much impact. My concerns about Good News for oppressed people must be forwarded through political action. But political action requires constant evaluation of the political scene and my Christian responsibility within that scene. I frankly find such Christianity to be intensely demanding of my time and energy. When I am looking around for what could be cut out of my busy schedule, it would be only too possible to fall into the activist form of anti-humanism, telling myself that there simply is not enough *time* or *money* to see good films, hear good concerts, or read and discuss good books (except for those with a directly contemporary political message).

In other words, it would be fatally easy to fall in with the prevalent assumption that the really *important* concerns of our time are economic, political, and technological, and that they are in no way illuminated by such frills as Greek drama, seventeenth-century poetry, and nineteenth-century novels. That mistake could rob me, not only of the stimulation and relaxation I need as a human being, but also of the reinforcement I need to remember what really matters in life. The timeless concerns of great art (including the Bible) provide the best guidance for setting priorities in the timely choices of everyday living.

"Burnout" is very common among contemporary activists. I think that the basic cause of "burnout" is trying to save the world single-handedly, constant *going* without adequate time for *getting ready* (speech, the word, ideological nurturance) and *getting set* (meditation and quiet centering, simply *being,* the subject of Part Two of this book). There is also something to be said for communal support and simple enjoyment.

I recently had a very significant dream. I was holding a baby while attending a convention in which the meetings were very long, serious, and intense. The baby, who looked a lot like my own baby pictures, sat quietly in my arms for many hours, but finally puckered up her face and began to cry lustily. I held her at arm's length and said unsympathetically, "What's the matter with *you?*" Although she was far too young to be able to talk, with the logical illogic of dreams she was able to give me a very direct answer: "After all these meetings, I feel like an abstract." Since the dream occurred when I was close to "burnout," I found the interpretation easy enough. The baby in me needed some attention; I was working too hard and needed to make time for some fun.

But as I thought more about the dream, I became impressed with the academic meaning of the word *abstract.* A scholarly abstract is a brief description of the main points of an article or book, so brief that it omits everything except the most important conclusions. All illustrations, all human interest materials, and the whole chain of concrete evidence that substantiates those conclusions—all these things are omitted. So I realized that not only was my unconscious mind warning me to get more rest and relaxation; it was also telling me that I was doing too much traveling around giving out my conclusions in speeches and spending too little time growing and deepening through reading and engaging in supportive conversation and simple human experience.

I hope that I will strike a better balance in the future so that I will not wind up feeling like an abstract again. And I hope that the church in the 1980s will not make the error either of total spiritualistic withdrawal or of plunging back into an activism that would leave the whole church community feeling like one great big abstract. We need to act out Christian concern for others. But we also need to make time for the arts in our lives. And we need to encourage the formal study of the humanities as a way of keeping our priorities humanized and teaching ourselves how to think clearly and feel humanely. In that way we can hope to choose sensibly in the political, biological, technological, and economic supermarket of the future.

We cannot be truly kind to others unless we learn to be kind to our own humanity, to the infant we hold in our arms.

4
Doing Justice
by Suspending Judgment:
A Case for Pluralism

By the early 1970s the books I was choosing to read were more and more centered on issues of justice. Erskine Caldwell, Richard Wright, William Faulkner, and James Baldwin got me sufficiently stirred up that I began to investigate injustices to American black people. My first social-justice essay was entitled "Up from Ignorance: Awareness-Training and Racism." After it appeared in *Christianity Today*, I got my first hate mail and discovered that people sometimes strike back when their consciences are pricked. Not long thereafter, I began to be sensitized about justice for women, and since then have been engaged in various justice-causes that seem an authentic response to the "still, small voice" within my nature.

In one of his editorials for *The Other Side: A Magazine of Christian Discipleship*, John Alexander told about an occasion in his youth when he had stuttered very badly and his older brother had enjoyed a good laugh at his expense. Alexander, feeling that lightning should have struck his brother for his heartlessness, thinks that his own commitment to human justice dates from that moment. Until the time of reading the editorial, I had not stopped to think much about where my own rage for justice had its origin; but the source was not hard to trace. Like John Alexander's, my concern for the underdog was developed in my youth by the experience of *being* an underdog, and specifically through the massive insensitivity of my older brother.

I was a fat baby, thirteen and a half pounds at birth and gaining all the way. By contrast, Bob was skin and bones despite the fact that he ate tremendous quantities of Hershey's kisses and Tastycake chocolate cupcakes. Although my mother did her best to treat us equally, my propensity to gain weight from the least bit of cake or candy forced her to ration my supplies stringently, whereas Bob's supply was virtually open-ended. I would sit next to him listening to "The Lone Ranger" on our console radio, enviously and hungrily watching him pop goodies into his mouth. As if that weren't bad enough, it was Bob's chief delight to remind me constantly about how fat I really was. Whenever neighborhood kids chimed "Fatso," my brother's voice would be leading the pack.

It did not seem fair. Bob could eat inordinately much and remain thin, while my eating was seriously restricted and I remained fat. Never a day went by that I was not reduced to tears by Bob's insistent teasing. Sometimes even my father would join in. I remember especially one very painful time when Dad teased me about being his little tub, and I burst into tears at this betrayal from my adored tower of strength. Not realizing how wounded I was, he teased me some more about crying, then got irritated because I didn't stop and ordered me to be a good sport and wipe my eyes. When I couldn't comply, he told me to sit in the corner for an hour—and my mother did nothing to interfere. I sat there raging with the injustice of it all. And I believe that some of the passion for justice which I have always felt, and which I now channel into writing, speaking, and acting on behalf of oppressed persons, was born that afternoon and nurtured throughout that humiliating childhood.

Although my mother never teased me about my weight, she added to my oppression by the intensity of her concern over it. I was so eager to please her that I was fully toilet trained before I was one year old; yet my appearance, I knew, was a continual affliction to her. Whenever it was time for new clothes, there would be the excruciating trip to the chubby shops, and afterward there would be clucking from my grandmother and aunts as the dresses were hemmed. Their size was discussed as if I were either deaf or unable to comprehend the grief I was causing to everyone. I learned to avert my eyes from mirrors and always experienced revulsion if I happened to catch my reflection in a store window. I was constantly hungry for sweets. And since a sweet dessert in our home was implicitly understood as a reward for being good, the fact that Bob could have so many more sweets than I meant to me that he was not only biologically but also morally superior to me.

It did not get much better as I grew older, except that people stopped mocking me to my face. All my life I have been on one diet after another, sometimes depriving myself so rigidly that I would come close to fainting and would spend day after day dragging myself to work without the energy natural to my body when I am consuming sufficient fat. But there was no significant response on the scales.

Everywhere I turned I was told—in magazines, on billboards, on the radio, on TV, in school—that there is only one cause of obesity, and that is *eating too much.* Society made many jokes at the expense of people like me: "The best exercise for weight loss is to lay down the fork, push the chair back from the table, and shake the head slowly from side to side." But I wasn't laughing. I knew that I was doing that "exercise" far sooner than many of my svelte friends. To no avail.

I sought help from medical doctors, of course, who put me on various diets guaranteed to make me lose weight if only I would stick to them faithfully. I stuck to them faithfully, all right. But when the scales did not show the expected weight loss, the doctors would look at me with tolerant amusement, or distrust, or sometimes even with anger. They simply could not believe that I had not cheated; and their disbelief felt degrading, dehumanizing, and utterly demoralizing.

Shortly after the birth of my son, I began to read widely in the field of nutrition. One day, in desperation because I was light-headed from my latest reducing diet, I wrote to the famous nutritionist Adelle Davis. She sent me a diet that consisted of several ounces of lean meat and salad but included no more than one teaspoon of oil a day. I perserved on that diet for months, despite the fact that I felt terrible and lost very little weight after the first two weeks. Only after I had developed extreme diarrhea, rapid heart, and chronic insomnia did I become frightened enough to give up on that diet. Although I spent enormous time and money trying to rid myself of those terrifying symptoms, it was six months before I got a decent night's sleep again, and even longer before my pulse began to normalize. And I was still fat.

On another occasion, I went to an expensive nutritionist in New York City who assured me that if I would concentrate on eating whole-grained foods and fresh fruits and vegetables, my weight would take care of itself because my body would be healthy. That sounded fine to me, since after reading Frances Lappe's *Diet for a Small Planet* I had felt guilty for eating so much meat. I wanted very badly to eat "lower on the food chain" in order to leave more food for others. So I happily followed instructions—and gained weight spectacularly.

In the course of much reading and many other futile attempts, I finally found an approach that worked for me: the approach taken by Dr. Robert Atkins in his *Dr. Atkins' Diet Revolution* and subsequent books. By following a diet of extremely low carbohydrates with almost unlimited proteins and fats, over a period of several years I was able to lose eighty-five pounds while feeling energetic and happy. But I was still overweight, and having reached "dead end," I decided to visit Dr. Atkins in person. I also took my son for treatment, since he seemed to have the same metabolic problems as I. After extensive testing, Dr. Atkins found that Paul and I did have similar metabolisms, although my problems were more serious than Paul's. Both of us were unable to handle more than about twenty-five grams of carbohydrates daily without experiencing dramatic weight gain. Although most people can *lose* weight on an intake of sixty carbohydrate grams daily, I can lose only when my intake is about ten to fifteen grams (and even one stick of sugar-free gum carries a gram of carbohydrate!).

Both my son and I turned out to be hypoglycemic (that

is, we have low blood sugar). And I had a hyperinsulin reaction to boot. The nurses and Dr. Atkins could not understand why I had not fainted during my glucose tolerance tests, so rapidly had my blood sugar plummeted. But having lived through forty-three years of forcing myself to continue functioning despite hunger and low blood-sugar symptoms, I was used to the grin-and-bear-it routine.

Now, several years later, I am still overweight but still about eighty-five pounds below the all-time high I had maintained for so many years before discovering the Atkins diet. Nothing I have been able to do, and nothing Dr. Atkins could think of trying, could get the scales to budge much further without heroic measures (such as eating nothing at all). The moment I began to eat even close to normally on the Atkins maintenance plan, my weight would return to approximately its present level. So I suppose I will have to live with things as they are. I cannot eat foods made with refined sugar and only very rarely foods that use honey, and I have to limit severely my intake of carbohydrates, including the natural sugars and starches in most fruits and vegetables. It will no doubt always be that way. By following the Atkins diet, my son, who is now twenty-one, has been able to lose over one hundred pounds; but he too will have to severely limit carbohydrate intake all of his life.

For me the greatest irony of this story is the amount of supportive encouragement I received during the time that the weight was dropping away. People actually began to perceive that I *did* have will power and integrity after all. From my point of view, of course, the time when I needed trust and affirmation was during all those years when I dieted with painfully rigid honesty, to no avail. While I was dieting successfully, the scales and mirror gave me all the affirmation I needed. But where was everybody when nothing was working for me?

Being fat was not the only stigma I grew up with, but it was the one which taught me on a day-to-day basis what it is to be treated as something considerably less than human. In our society obese persons are not taken seriously. They are trivialized by acquaintances who can lose weight by simple self-restraint and therefore assume that obesity is always a matter of gluttony or at least self-indulgence. *Some* obesity is exactly that; for instance, anybody who can lose weight on the Weight Watchers program is probably a person who has simply overeaten because of psychological pressures or what-have-you. People with metabolisms like mine would gain enormous poundage by eating as much carbohydrate as Weight Watchers recommends!

Recently, fat people have been assaulted by new and even more demoralizing attacks on their dignity. Feminists are saying that fat is a feminist issue, a sign of self-hatred fostered by a sexist society. Psychologists are claiming that fatness is an attempt to repudiate sexuality by shrouding oneself in "ugly fat." Charismatic Christians are saying that fat is a spiritual issue, indicating a lack of submission to the will of God. Many claim that healing from fatness is available to anyone who has sufficient faith—so those who remain fat after joining the healing lines must now add a sense of faithlessness to their sense of unattractiveness! Radical evangelicals are saying that in a world of widespread poverty and hunger, fatness is a sign of sinful selfishness. And medical doctors continue to say that there is only one cause of overweight—overeating—despite a mounting pile of evidence that many overweight people eat much less than their thinner friends and acquaintances.

Apart from a passionate identification with oppressed and stigmatized people, the main thing I have learned from my most obvious stigma is to suspend judgment about other people. I sense that when some people look at me, they think to themselves, "Why doesn't she care enough about her witness to diet a little and lose some weight?" (Like black-, red-, or yellow-skinned people, fat people cannot hide their stigma.) I sense that when some of my radical evangelical colleagues see me eating beef, they think to themselves, "She certainly would make a better witness for justice if she restrained herself from consuming food that is so expensive and so high on the food chain." So when I catch myself looking at somebody else and beginning to pass negative judgment about some aspect of their looks or their behavior, I try to make an instant mental correction. How do *I* know what life is like for them?

A related lesson I have learned is the importance of *pluralism.* Instead of assuming that other people are or ought to be just like myself and instead of trying to force my behavior patterns on them, I have learned that I need to respect their individual differences (and I'm talking about *actual* respect, not just lip service). There is *not* just one cause of overweight; there are many causes. Nutritionist Linda Clark is probably right that obesity is on the increase in the United States because people's bodies are undernourished. So many supermarket foods are stripped of their nutritional content by high-heat processes and chemical substitutions that many people are eating more and more, unconsciously trying to get the basic nutrients their bodies crave.

A highly respected nutritional researcher, Dr. William Kelley, has found that there are at least *ten* different metabolic types. *First,* there are strict vegetarian types who can live comfortably on fruits, vegetables, and nuts and who get groggy when they eat meat. *Second*, there are nonstrict vegetarians who need about four ounces of animal protein daily to feel their best. *Third*, there are poorly metabolizing vegetarians who need 30 percent more food a day than other people just in order to maintain the same weight and sense of well-being. *Fourth*, there are extremely carnivorous people who feel better when they eat meat every day, and need and enjoy butter and cream (apparently this is the category Paul and I fit into). *Fifth*, there are the nonextreme carnivorous persons who need meat but can go without it for several days without feeling negative effects. *Sixth*, there are meat-eaters with poor metabolisms who need a much greater volume of food to maintain the same weight and sense of wellbeing as others. *Seventh*, there are people who need a balance of meat and vegetables but metabolize so poorly that they can absorb only 10 to 15 percent of what they eat. Consequently, they can eat enormous amounts of food without gaining weight. *Eighth*, there are people who can look and feel good eating normal amounts of anything at all as long as it's reasonably nutritious. *Ninth*, there are people similar to those in category eight except that they crave cooked food and are uncomfortable with raw food. To feel good, they need to eat at least 70 percent of their food cooked. *Tenth*, there are the superefficient metabolizers who need very small amounts of food and very little sleep. They can eat half as much as normal people and still feel satisfied and full of pep. (People who desire further information may write to *The Healthview Newsletter*, 612 Rio Road West, Box 6670, Charlottesville, Virginia 22906.)

It should be obvious, in the light of such findings, how ridiculous and even cruel it may be for persons in one category to pass judgment on persons in another. Human metabolisms, like almost everything else about human bodies and personalities, are full of variety. We do serious injustice to others when we try to make ourselves the single norm to which they must measure up.

Some years ago, before I lost my eighty-five pounds, I was with a group of people of various faiths, united by our common interest in meditation and spiritual growth. We were watching the classic silent film of the trial of Joan of Arc. Concerning the clerics who were condemning Joan to the flames, the moderator commented, "Just look at their fat, cruel faces as opposed to Joan's slender, spiritual form!" I was, of course, depressed by this equation of fatness with evil and thinness with spirituality, and it occurred to me that I was getting a taste of what my black brothers and sisters endure all the time. I was glad that my son was not there to hear it. And I smiled ruefully when I recalled that the same moderator who had revealed his fat-phobia by equating fatness with evil was an ardent admirer of Pope John XXIII, whom he called "the most saintly man I ever met"—and he had met the Dalai Lama, Albert Schweitzer, and plenty of other candidates for that distinction! Yet Pope John XXIII could hardly have been called slender!

I hope that serious Christians in the 1980s will make a concerted effort to move toward nonjudgmental acceptance and affirmation of human diversity and pluralism. We human beings are one in the New Creation; yet we are all different. So be it.

PART TWO: SILENCE

5
Learning to Live in the Wind

If you entered a Plymouth Brethren "morning meeting," which is the Communion service, you would probably be reminded of what you have heard about Quaker meetings. People sit in silence around the Lord's Table, and from time to time a man will get up from his seat to "give out" a hymn, or to lead in prayer, or to read a passage of Scripture, or to explicate that Scripture. No one plans these meetings in advance, but you come to understand after a few of them that things will move toward the breaking of the bread and the drinking of the wine, after which the offering will be taken and announcements made before a final hymn and prayer. Which of the brethren will initiate the actual "breaking of bread" is not prescheduled, for no one is ordained. Everything is left to the guidance of the Holy Spirit, except that it is clearly understood that the Holy Spirit would never lead a woman to participate audibly. Sometimes the silences would grow to a length of two or three minutes; but I noticed that people always seemed to feel the meeting was a better one if there was very little silence and things moved along at a brisk pace.

Since I spent my first twenty-five years attending such meetings, you might well suppose that I developed some expertise in the art of contemplation. Alas, it was not so. No one ever gave us youngsters any indication of how to meditate during those silent periods. My mother told me, when I was four or five, that I should be "thinking about what Jesus had done for me on the cross," and I tried. God knows I tried. But there is a big difference between forcing the mind to reconstruct, over and over, the few facts it has gleaned about an event like the crucifixion, and entering into creative meditation, whether of the structured or the "wisely passive" variety. Perhaps it would have been different had I possessed a native gift for contemplation. As it was, I doodled on scraps of paper tucked into my Bible, or I looked at other people, or I put in time worrying about catching the germs of a woman who never stopped coughing for more than five minutes and yet drank out of the common cup. Once I began to develop sexually, I discovered that there was never any lack of material to "meditate" about. All of this was of no assistance in learning the disciplined focus of the mind, which is required for contemplative prayer and meditation. I suspect, in fact, that asking children to sit in silence may well be counterproductive, encouraging them in undisciplined self-entertainment that has to be unlearned before any real meditation can take place. At any rate, silencing my "ego-babble" is still the hardest thing I have to do in my daily life, and I am far from adept at it.

As I understood what I heard at home and in the Assembly, prayer was a structured matter of *talking to God.* So for many years I tried to carry out a pattern that now seems futile at best, rude at worst. By *rude* I mean this: I would never dream of corralling another human being to sit down alone with me to listen while I talked nonstop at him or her, never pausing for so much as a one-word reaction let alone *listening* for what that other individual might have to say to me in return. Yet that is how I understood prayer for many years. I was treating God with less respect than I would show an employee who worked for me full time. Any answer God might have for me, I expected to come by way of *action.* He—and God was definitely male to my imagination— would give me what I asked for, or he would give me something else instead, and that was his "answer." Whether I was asking things for myself or others, or whether I was praising God or thanking God, or whatever I was doing, all the communication was cognitive, a constant flow of *words,* and all one-way. Speech, not silence.

Most of the discussion of prayer I had ever heard centered on whether God answers prayer and how we can know that he does. But during the past decade I have come to believe that prayer is not a matter of *my* calling in an attempt to get God's attention, but of my finally *listening to the call of God,* which has been constant, patient, and insistent in my inner being. In relationship to God, I am not the seeker, the initiator, the one who loves more greatly. In prayer, as in the whole salvation story unfolded by Scripture, God is reaching out to me, speaking to me, and it is up to me to learn to be polite enough to pay attention. When I do have something to say to God, I am rendering a response to the divine

initiative. So the questions of whether or not and how
God answers prayer now seem to me bogus questions.
God speaks, all right. The big question is do *I* answer, do
I respond, to an invitation that is always open.

I do not mean to imply that I have no use for liturgical
or communal prayer, which serves as a concrete
enactment of my oneness with the other members of the
family of God. But I know, and I think every honest
person knows, that communal prayers are sometimes
real to my inner experience, and sometimes not, and that
the difference lies in the kind of internal focus I am able
to give to them. I think that those who attack traditional
liturgy, ritual, and communal prayer as meaningless to
modern humanity are bogging themselves down in a
great muddle. Religious communal celebrations enact,
reinforce, and incarnate the human sense of mortal
interrelationship, divine interrelationship, and divine-
human interrelationship.

I also have no intention of denying the value of
intercessory prayer. Only for me at this stage of my life,
intercessory prayer is no longer ticking off a list of people
and dictating to God what I think God ought to do for
them. Increasingly, for me, interceding is remembering
the presence of God and then remembering the persons
I'm concerned about *in* the remembered presence of
God. If those persons are sick, I try to envision them in
radiant health, but at the same time I sense that I do not
really know their best interests. (How could I, when I am
not even sure about my own best interests?) So I have to
offer my concern in a listening, open fashion.

I wonder whether intercessory prayer might not be a
matter of transmitting positive energy to other human
beings by entering deeply into the One Spirit who moves
through both my deepest self and theirs. No matter how

far away those persons I am praying for may be, and whether or not they are known to me personally, they are not outside of that One Spirit (that Christ-nature), which is the source, essence, and support of our mutual existence. So in the profound energy field that we share, perhaps my poured-out concern is transmitted into benefit for those whose need has been brought home to my silent spirit. Could that be something of what is meant by praying in the "name" of Jesus?

Those who are advanced in contemplation, meditation, and prayer will recognize without my telling them that I am only a neophyte. It is not my intention to pose as an authority on the interior life, but rather to share the faith-journey of my recent years and to think about its implications for the future. (As Robert Browning wrote in another connection, "God uses us to help each other so, / Lending our minds out.")

Since my direction has been dual, toward greater silence on the one hand and toward activism on the other, I am trying to explain something of the process by which I arrived at my current understanding of the faith experience. Precisely because contemplation is so foreign to my early experience and because I have had to struggle so hard to learn the little I do know, it may be that my experience will be helpful to someone else. I remember hearing in an undergraduate education course that sometimes the most brilliant scholars do not make the best teachers. They are *so* brilliant—grasp ideas and methods with such lightning rapidity—that they lack the patience to teach other people the step-by-step process most people need. In some cases people of genius cannot even grasp the reality of the ordinary person's need for methodical continuity. Having so directly intuited a correct theory, the genius may perceive a continuum where the rest of us perceive only a frustrating gap. If that is true, then the fact that contemplative prayer comes so hard for me may even prove to be an advantage.

My "journey into silence" began, I think, with a very significant dream. I was walking in a city, in a small brick square at the front of a cathedral. On the steps of the cathedral, which was just to my right, stood an angel with golden eyelids, looking at me with infinitely tender loving-kindness. The angel wore a white robe, but I do not remember any wings or halo or even an aura, just those golden eyelids. I had a distinct impression of androgyny, however, and I was certain that this was an angel and that he/she took a loving interest in my welfare, although no words were spoken. Suddenly I looked out to my left and saw some heavy storm clouds with a cyclone beginning to dip down out of the cloud formations. Across the square, I saw some wooden picnic tables and noticed that some people had already taken refuge from the tornado by getting under the tables. In alarm, I looked to the angel, who directed me with her/his hand to seek shelter with the others under the table. End of dream.

At first I simply reveled in the sense of divine love that filled me when I awoke. But I thought long and hard about that angel with the golden eyelids. As I became interested in psychological androgyny, of course, I couldn't help remembering that "my angel" was somehow both male and female without seeming the least bit freakish—but then, I could have picked that idea up from Milton, whose Muse is androgynous and whose angels can assume any shape at all. One day when I was lying on my back in the sun with my eyes closed, I realized that *my own eyelids were golden* because of the sun I was basking in. And it came to me that on one level, the dream was telling me that I should stop being so distrustful of my own interior experience, that some of my best guidance would come from relating to God within my own spirit.

But for quite a while I continued to assume that the storm was necessarily a negative symbol, and I continued to wonder off and on about what meaning I was supposed to draw from hiding under a flimsy picnic table in the face of a cyclone. Only during the past few months (as a result of another dream) have I related the cyclone to the whirlwind presence of God in the Bible.

Why, then, hide under a table in fear of that presence? One day when I was busy thinking about something else, suddenly I remembered the Canaanite woman who changed the mind of Jesus about healing her daughter by reminding him, when he refused because she wasn't Jewish, that even dogs are allowed to eat the crumbs that fall from the master's table (Matt. 15:21-28). Whenever I heard that story as a child, I always envisioned a long wooden table similar to the picnic tables of my dream. Like that woman whose determination saved her daughter's life, I was being instructed to trust boldly in my perception of the extension of God's love and power to people ordinarily considered beyond inclusion in that love or that power, and to identify myself with them (get under the same table). Not long after the dream, I had, in fact, identified myself first with the Evangelical Women's Caucus, where women struggled for the power to become all they were meant to be, and then with Evangelicals Concerned, a national task force of homosexuals and heterosexuals working together for a better understanding of homosexuality in the Christian community.

I am impressed by how many of the themes of my past few years are summarized by the various levels of that dream: first, the increasing interiority (the golden eyelids, a sense of God's *immanence* on my own pulses), followed by the awareness of the sweeping power of what God is doing in contemporary history (the tornado, the sense of God's *transcendence* on my own pulses). And then the sense that although I have felt myself to be an outsider and a loner in many ways, I need to join myself in community (under the table) in order to be able to respond to the terrific force of God's presence in contemporary society. And the sense that the tables are properly not within the cathedral, not inside the vested interests of human institutions, but out there in the streets of the city, the locus of human need; and the sense that I am to identify myself with the oppressed. And that despite my interest in other religions, especially despite the fact that I continue to learn so much from oriental religion and philosophy, the place for me continues to be under the table of Jesus. It is from precisely this angle that I (being who I am) can catch authentic glimpses of the Fields of Light. I know that the "bright shoots of everlastingness" are perceived by other people from other angles: from a Zen Buddhist perspective, perhaps, or from a Jewish one. I am glad to share the unitive *experience* with others without feeling forced to arrive at *doctrinal agreement* with them. Here again, I will not try to dictate to God's Spirit how to work within other persons. I will try instead to be a faithful witness to what *I* am taught "under the table," at the feet of Jesus.

I realize how far out what I have just said may sound to people from backgrounds similar to my own. I well remember how afraid I was to accept the possibility that truth could come to me from any source other than one which had the Protestant version of an *imprimatur* upon it. Or that truth could come to people of other religions without their conscious, cognitive acceptance of the doctrines of the Christian faith. After all, Jesus said that nobody could come to the Father except by him (John 14:6). And referring to Jesus, Peter had said, "There is no other name under heaven granted to men, by which we may receive salvation" (Acts 4:12 NEB). But when confronted by passages like "Abraham put his faith in God, and that faith was counted to him as righteousness" (Rom. 4:3 NEB), I began to see other possibilities. Certainly Abraham had never consciously heard the name of Jesus Christ, but his faith in God's unique encounter with himself was "counted to him as righteousness." Could it be possible that coming to the Father "by Jesus" might mean coming to the Father *in the same way Jesus came,* with full confidence in loving relationship and unswerving determination to carry out the divine will?

Initially, it was I Corinthians 13:12 that opened my mind to such possibilities; for if each of us sees only "puzzling reflections in a mirror," then none of us is wise to reject another person over a difference of perception. This is important because knowledge, including all our theories, is defined as passing away with time, whereas love is eternal. And none of us is wise to reject insights because they come from an unorthodox source.

I was helped further by Percy Bysshe Shelley's version of a similar insight, in *Adonais:*

> Life, like a dome of many-coloured glass,
> Stains the white radiance of Eternity,
> Until Death tramples it to fragments.

Since metaphorically we human beings all exist under a many-colored bell jar, our perceptions will depend on our own experiences and temperaments, which will inevitably color the way we see and talk about reality. This is not to say that there is no *objective* "white radiance of Eternity"; it *is* to say that no mortal mind is wise to flatter itself that it has taken in the entire spectrum and mixed all the colors together in the perfect combination to produce an accurate perception of objective reality. Although Matthew Arnold urges us to "see life steadily and see it whole," we had better remember that part of the condition of being human is that we are unable to do so for any length of time. To switch to one of Milton's *Areopagitica* metaphors, Truth is such a constantly flowing fountain that whenever any individual tries to wall off part of it as a permanent private possession, the result can only be a stagnant pool cut off from the flow of the living Source (cf. John 4:10-15; John 3:8).

Personally, I want to be where the water is flowing freely and where the wind is blowing as it will.

6
A Course in Miracles

About three years ago I was sitting in a New York restaurant with my sister-in-law Marilyn, talking about the fact that my son, then eighteen, showed very little interest in academic studies and did not want to go to college. I admitted that, as a college teacher myself, I was sometimes troubled by Paul's lack of scholarly concern and that once in a while the thought would cross my mind, "Since I was to have only one child, why couldn't that child have shared more of my interests?" Marilyn said, "You know what you're really saying? You're angry at God for not giving you the kind of child you think you should have had." Instantly I knew in my heart that she was right and asked where she had derived such an insight. She told me about a remarkable set of books she had been given by a friend of hers, called *A Course in Miracles*. I asked her to get me a set, which she promised to bring the next time we got together.

During the month or so that intervened before I got my own copy of "the course," I pondered my attitude about my son's academic unconcern. And I realized that I had felt anger at God because I thought it was in my best interest to have a scholarly child, and God had let me down. As I thought further about Paul's personality, I began to realize gratefully that he is just the perfect son for me to have: gentle, strong, humanly concerned, loving, very bright about machinery and those things that capture *his* attention, and very proud of me for doing those things that capture *my* interest. After several weeks of perceiving Paul in this new light, I began to notice that Paul was acting more comfortable in my presence than he had for some time. I was astonished when he wrote on his Mother's Day card that he was proud of me for the way I was "learning to love"—astonished because I had never *said* I was disappointed with his academic disinterest and therefore had never told him that now I was happy with him just the way he was. But he *knew*; and he gave me a gift of affirmation in return for my affirmation of him. The silent healing that took place in our relationship remains steady till this day; so I had experienced my first "miracle" even before I had had a chance to study *A Course in Miracles*.

The first time I actually got my hands on the course, I read far into the night. I was impressed by its clear-cut distinction between *miracle* and *magic*. Magic occurs, I learned, when someone helpless is "healed" through the agency of someone else who supposedly has special and unique access to the power of God. Magic is also involved when persons attempt to place their reliance in themselves alone as separated beings and seem to be successful at it. By contrast, miracles are a way of giving acceptance to others and simultaneously receiving it, since in reality (because of human oneness) giving and receiving are the same. Miracles are the acts of faith of a son or daughter of God who has laid aside false gods, who recognizes that all human beings can do the same, and who therefore speaks directly to the Christ-Mind or eternal Self in everyone. The distinction reminded me of the fact that Jesus repeatedly located the impetus of healing power in the person he had healed: "*Your faith has saved you.*"

Miracles therefore do not instill awe, but rather instill love between equals: "The power of one mind can shine into another, because all the lamps of God were lit by the same spark" (*Text*, p. 175). I had already experienced enough of a healing miracle with my own son to know that this statement was true. The Christ-Mind in Paul is perfect, absolutely perfect. So is the Christ-Mind in me. When we speak to this in one another there is an exquisitely tender respect and mutuality that lights up our whole relationship.

In the following weeks and months as I studied the course, I discovered that it asks both everything and nothing of me. It asks nothing in the sense that I am asked to give up only those fearful illusions that block my awareness of Love's presence as the ultimate and only reality in the universe. But it asks everything in the sense that I must learn to recognize the insanity of all my ideas of personal specialness, all the delusions that I am somehow either better or worse than the rest of God's creatures. It asks me to believe that God has only one Offspring—the entire real creation—which is beloved as a unit and therefore is loved equally, absolutely, and utterly by its Progenitor. From the egotistical standpoint, to believe that is asking a great deal, because as W. H. Auden phrased it, the "error bred in the bone" is that we want "not universal love, but to be loved alone." Or to shift to T. S. Eliot's phrasing, *A Course in Miracles* offers me "A condition of complete simplicity (costing not less than everything)."

According to the course, the idea that God's Offspring could fall into objectively real sin and death is a delusion spun by the destructive ego-consciousness. Why? In order to engender guilty fear of the love of God and thus assure the survival of the ego (in New Testament language, "the old nature"). The course explains that it is impossible for the Offspring of God to leave God's mind (in God "we live, and move, and have our being" Acts 17:28 KJV). It is thus impossible for God's Offspring to effectually differentiate herself or himself from God and thus to effectually oppose God's will. It is therefore also impossible for the self that the ego imagines—and the world that the ego makes by its own projections—to become the master of God's Offspring.

I readily admit that I am still in the process of trying to sort out the teachings of *A Course in Miracles* against the standard I consider normative, the Bible. Although I have serious difficulty with some of the concepts, I have tried not to use my cognitive hesitations to shield me from the healing growth that the course offers, even to those whose belief is less than total. I can testify that through its insights I have been brought to acknowledge that the world I see at any moment is determined by who I think I am at that moment and by what I believe to be the relationship of others to myself. Often kicking and screaming inside because of my desire to evade responsibility, I have been brought to the point of placing responsibility for my world view where it belongs: on myself. What I see is what I am. I see the world as I choose to see it; so if I regard another person as my enemy, I must acknowledge my responsibility for that perception rather than placing the blame on the other person for what I perceive. Such a realization is disconcerting at first, but later feels utterly liberating. Once I know that I am the cause of my own misery, I know that I do not have to *remain* miserable. If I am willing to allow my perceptions to be cleansed, the Holy Spirit will teach me to see with Christ's own happy-making vision.

I have discovered that my entire view of things changes (as a whole unit, an entire Gestalt) when I look at things from the standpoint of my body-identified, localized ego-consciousness as opposed to when I look at things from the standpoint of "Christ in me." Although by nature I feel contented most of the time, I am never entirely free of fear (in dozens of masked forms, but all of them lacking in love) as long as I let myself believe that I am separated from God and from other beings.

Since God created the One Offspring by self-extension, then God's will and the Offsprings' will (that is, the human will in the *real, eternal Self*) are actually *one will*. When I choose to side with my false self and its body-identified ego-delusions (such as that I am separate from you, that you owe me happiness, that my interests are more important than your interests), I experience a split consciousness that causes deep conflict within me. I will then try to evade the self-disgust this conflict causes by resenting other people for failing to meet my ego-needs and by passing judgment upon them. As the course textbook puts it: "You are afraid to know God's will, because you believe it is not yours. This belief is your whole sickness and your whole fear. Every symptom of sickness and fear arises here, because this is the belief that makes you *want* not to know. Believing this you hide in darkness, denying that the light is in you" (p. 182).

Each time I reread the course, I am struck by the quietly confident, soft-spoken tone of it. When first I saw it, the combination of casual peacefulness and authority in the opening sentences made my eyes widen: "This is a course in miracles. It is a required course. Only the time you take it is voluntary." And nearly twelve hundred pages later I still found the same quiet assurance that had never deviated throughout: "The Holy Spirit abides in the part of your mind that is part of the Christ Mind. He represents your Self and your Creator, Who are one. He speaks for God and also for you, being joined with both. . . . He seems to be a Voice, for in that form He speaks God's Word to you. . . . He seems to be whatever meets the need you think you have. But He is not deceived when you perceive your self entrapped in needs you do not have. It is from these He would deliver you" (*Teacher's Manual,* p. 85). Having already been freed from entrapment to the need I thought I had for a scholarly son, I was inclined to take all of this very much to heart. I still am, for it would be impossible to describe how often relationships have been eased or frustrations have been dissolved by applying these principles.

I came to realize that when the course utilizes the first person, the "I" is the voice of Jesus, who refers to himself as the elder brother. This voice claims that the proper response to him is love between equals rather than awe (because "awe implies inequality"). More importantly, this voice explains that the difference between him and me is that he *has* and *is* nothing except what comes from God, whereas that state is only potential in me. He has transcended all limitation; he has overcome death, which is the symbol of the fear of God; he has recognized himself as God's self-extension, and by doing so has recognized all living things as part of him. He is the Savior, the Christ, because he saw the false without accepting it as true. But he assures me that "there is nothing about me that you cannot attain" (*Text*, p. 5), even though the final step to that attainment is God's move, a move belonging to the larger Process/Pattern rather than to me as one segment of that Process/Pattern.

Although from the point of view of my doctrinal background such assurances make my knees unsteady, still I have *experienced* the course as a step-by-step manual toward Christ-like maturity. And I am struck by a certain similarity to Romans 8:29: "For God knew his own before ever they were, and also ordained that they should be shaped to the likeness of his Son, that he might be the eldest among a large family of brothers" (NEB).

As a feminist I am keenly aware that some of the women among my readers will feel excluded by the masculine language of the New English Bible passage I have just quoted. Such readers would also be upset by the male pronouns and imagery of the course itself. Although I have been speaking of the course concepts in inclusive language as much as possible, the fact is that it speaks of the Father (not the Progenitor) and the Son (not the Offspring), and speaks of all males and females and indeed the whole creation as part of one single Sonship. As I think you will see from my discussion of God-language, I certainly do not consider the language issue a trivial one. Like the philosopher Wittgenstein, I believe that the limits of my language are the limits of my world. However, I am also aware that the English language presents very special problems for any attempt to express the organic oneness of the whole human race through singular pronouns, which must be either masculine, feminine, or neuter. The neuter denies the living quality, and either the masculine or feminine singular seems to be denying the other half of the human race. English grammar, depending as it does on rules developed by patriarchal consciousness several centuries ago, dictates that the correct "generic" pronoun is masculine. That can be changed and must be changed, and eventually will be changed. I think it would have been more helpful, at this juncture in history, had the editor of the course chosen to take the plunge and make the language as inclusive as possible.

Nevertheless, I refuse to cut myself off from the rich meaning of the Sonship metaphor either in the course or in various mystical writings or in the New Testament itself. The word *Son* was chosen, I believe, to indicate a gradually equalizing relationship with the Father, as opposed to the inequality and utter dependency that are implied by the word *child.* And the word was *son* rather than *daughter,* because, let's face it, in the patriarchal culture out of which the New Testament came to us, the sons were the heirs. The Sonship image is intended to show us that we will gradually inherit what the Father is, as a son "becomes" his father through maturation and inheritance.

But the New Testament makes clear that both males *and females* are included in the Sonship by including both males and females in the other major metaphors of divine-human oneness, the metaphors of the Bride of Christ and the single Body of Christ. So neither in the New Testament, nor in *A Course in Miracles,* nor in any of the mystical writings I have been devouring during the past several years, will I allow myself to be cut off from the inclusive intention of the metaphor of Sonship.

Nonetheless, I try never to use that metaphor without explaining the language problem and the central intention as I understand it. I do not want ever to give the impression that I am wiping out my own womanhood and that of my sisters by my choice of language.

As I have come to understand it, the central thesis of *A Course in Miracles* is this: "Forgive the world, and you will come to understand that everything that God created cannot have an end, and nothing He did not create is real" (*Manual*, p. 50). Although that sounded confusingly abstract to me when I first read it, I have since experienced how powerfully concrete its implications are. For instance, suppose a friend (let's call him Charles) says something to me that sounds like a terrific put-down. My instant, natural reaction is to feel insulted. He had no right to say a thing like that to me! After all I've done for him! Certainly I'm not perfect, but I've done nothing bad enough to deserve *that!* And so help me, he's going to crawl before I'll forgive him for it!

But from the point of view taught by the course, either Charles consciously intended to hurt me or he didn't. If he didn't consciously intend to hurt me, then there is nothing to get angry about because the *insult* is not real. Charles and I can clarify our real feelings about each other and then get on with our friendship. On the other hand, if Charles really *did* intend to hurt me, then he was forgetting that he and I are both part of a single eternal Sonship, so that he has fallen into the error of striking out at himself. Clearly the Christ-Mind in Charles was not the source of that error; it was his old nature, his ego, that deluded him into attacking another person and thus reinforcing his own fears.

But the old nature is in fact dead, a delusion, a temporal error, which has no eternal reality. If I can keep from being deceived by my own old nature into treating Charles's nastiness as if it were real, I can continue to focus on what *is* real about Charles: the Christ-nature, the New Humanity. If, instead of striking back at Charles, I speak gently to the Holy Spirit in him, he may be reminded of who he is and be snapped out of his erroneous perception. In that case, we will be best of friends again in no time, because he will be sorry for his failure of perception, and I will be effortlessly forgiving because I will understand that he did nothing to me but only to himself.

On the other hand, Charles may choose to continue to give validity to his ego-delusions. In that case I still have lost nothing real, even if we never see each other again. In fact, by forgiving him in the way I have described, I will have done myself the favor of reminding myself that "everything that God created cannot have an end" (including the Christ-nature or true Self in Charles and me) and "nothing that He did not create is real" (including the old nature or false self in Charles and me). In a sense I can even feel grateful to Charles for providing me with the opportunity to remind myself of who I am (eternally real because of "Christ-in-me"). Hence by forgiving Charles I am reinforcing my own sense of what is real and what is not and am increasing my ability to forgive myself for my own frequent lapses into error.

The same principles apply to the more horrendous examples of human cruelty in the world. Nazis committed atrocities because they failed to remember the oneness of God's Offspring. Contemporary brutalities reported in our newspapers and depicted in films such as *The Deer Hunter* arise from the same failures of perception. When we look at the perpetrators of physical and psychological violence through the eyes of Love, we are able to say with

Christ, "Father, forgive them; *they do not know what they are doing*" (Luke 23:34 NEB). Italics mine.

Psychologists or pastors may be quick to point out that such principles are not unique, that they may be learned in dozens of places and need not be credited specifically to *A Course in Miracles*. And I would not dispute with them. Certainly since studying the course, I have seen many of its insights in dozens of other places, including the Bible and other literary works written many centuries before our own. But it was *A Course in Miracles* that brought it all into a meaningful configuration for me, so I simply am sharing that awareness. (People wanting further information may write to the Foundation for Inner Peace, Box 635, Tiburon, California 94920.)

I wish that I could say that I live constantly in the Holy Spirit and consistently speak to the Holy Spirit within others, never crowding them or failing to affirm their divine worth. I do not, but that is my goal. I am comforted to notice that even the apostle Paul experienced inner struggles like my own (recorded in Rom. 7). To those who have to put up with me when I am not properly centered in my true Self, the Christ-nature, the Spirit of the New Humanity, I can only echo the words of the popular lapel button: "Please be patient. God isn't finished with me yet."

7
The Political Implications of Religious Imagery

In her 1979 book *Changing of the Gods,* Naomi Goldenberg comments that "a woman's feelings about her body undergo joyous transformation if she imagines herself to be in some sense divine. Those who cast spells and work hexes know that thought has effects in the world—that thought *certainly* influences the one who casts the spells and works the hexes and that thought *seems* to operate on other things as well" (p. 126). Although I disagree with much of what Goldenberg says elsewhere in her book, I think she is absolutely accurate about the power of *imagining.* As I imagine, so I think. As I think, so I act. As I act, so I am. As I am, so I perceive. Many religious leaders, such as Norman Vincent Peale, have emphasized the immense power of positive thinking; so that in itself is nothing new. What has not been adequately dealt with, however, is the *political* effect of how we *imagine God to look.*

It is precisely because of the power of imagining that
the language issue is of such importance to feminists.
Through many centuries, the God-language of worship
and liturgy has been a male language: God is the Father,
Christ Jesus is the Son, and even the Holy Spirit has been
referred to as either "him" or "it." Because of such
exclusively male image-making, males have received
implicit encouragement to identify themselves with the
divine. No matter how sophisticated I may be about the
process called anthropomorphism, my imagination is
going to give me a male picture when I call God my
Father. If I were male, this image or picture would
empower me to believe in myself, to be proud of my
body, and to have the courage of my convictions. Since I
am not male but female, that image or picture exerts
subtle pressure on me to give away my power to some
being other than myself, someone who more fully
resembles the picture in my imagination, someone *male*.
It is not probable that I will consciously realize what is
happening to me while it is happening. Even when the
enfeeblement process is pointed out to me, I may feel so
totally identified with my place in the only picture I can
currently imagine that I may hate the person who tries to
introduce anything different. For that reason certain
women have been by far the most virulent opponents of
Women's Liberation.

Because of this same power of the imagination, there is
a close relationship between the way we human beings
think and speak about God and the political structures of
the world in which we live. It is no accident that modern
power structures (hierarchical pyramids) mirror the way
we have thought and spoken about God as the High King
ruling over his archangels and lesser angels and human
creatures and animals and vegetation, all the way down

to the humblest clod of earth. That world-picture (in the Renaissance known as "the Great Chain of Being") has dominated society for centuries. National governments have similar chains of command, as do the military. Business corporations reflect the patriarchal God-picture in their hierarchies, and so do universities and churches. (Even though some religious groups like my own Plymouth Brethren Assemblies deny that they have any clerical hierarchy, it is only too evident that the Assemblies *do* have an implicit hierarchy, which makes some men more authoritative than others and all men more authoritative than women.) Traditionalists argue that the Christian home should reflect the same model, with the husband primary, the wife secondary, and the children tertiary.

So let us make no mistake about it: the way we think and speak about God is by no means a trivial matter. It has important personal repercussions, and for that very reason it has important political repercussions. A central task in the Christian struggle against the dehumanizing cruelty of this world's "cosmic powers . . . authorities and potentates" (Eph. 6:12 NEB) must therefore concern itself with changes in our personal, liturgical, and theological God-language.

For many Christian and Jewish persons, the things I have just been saying are too dangerous even to contemplate, because the patriarchal picture we have of God (the picture which has so empowered males and so enfeebled females) is rooted in the Bible. The most traditionally orthodox Jewish and Christian leaders refuse to budge an inch toward the acceptance of female imagery concerning the Godhead because they fear that once they do, that will be the end of Judaism and Christianity. Frequently, the same people also try to obstruct equal opportunities for women in business, government, clerical, and academic hierarchies. Perhaps they act not so much out of personal egotism as out of an intuition that political change could enforce changes in religious imagining and thus bring about the demise of the faith to which they are committed.

On that topic the most radical feminist thinkers entirely agree with the most orthodox traditionalists. For instance, the subtitle of Naomi Goldenberg's *Changing of the Gods* is *Feminism and the End of Traditional Religions.* Goldenberg is sure that "every woman working to improve her own position in society or that of women in general is bringing about the end of God" (p. 10)—and as far as she is concerned, that would be good riddance. She finds the work of Jewish and Christian feminists self-conflicted if not downright self-deceptive. If enough women came to represent God's authority in churches and synagogues, she insists, congregations would have to stop imagining God as male. And according to Goldenberg's understanding of things, such female religious officials could not possibly read the Bible with their congregations: "A society that accepted large numbers of women as religious leaders would be too different from the biblical world to find the book relevant, let alone look to it for inspiration" (p. 3).

If Goldenberg is right, then every man and woman who is deeply committed to human equality and social justice would be forced to follow Mary Daly's leadership by walking right out of Judaism or Christianity and into some type of free-form spirituality. But Dr. Daly's 1979 book, *Gyn-Ecology: The Metaethics of Radical Feminism,* already demonstrates the danger implicit in imaginative constructs that have no accountability to anything beyond the individual and her own ego-chosen community. Only a few years after her departure from Christianity, Daly has divinized just the female half of the human race, leaving the evil male half to fend for itself. That solution is just not radical enough; it is the same old hierarchy, only with subordinate and superordinate roles reversed. I do not want to continue living in a world in which exclusive depictions of God as a great Father and King empower males to dominate over females. But neither do I find it attractive to think about a world in which pictures of the divine as exclusively a Goddess/Mother/Queen empower females to aspire toward dominating over males. It is the *concept of dominance*, the whole idea of inflexible hierarchy, that I want liberation *from*. I want liberation *for* co-humanity, cooperation, coexistence, covenant, community.

And it is in the person and message of Christ Jesus that I have learned about that kind of liberation. As I tried to explain in my book *Women, Men, & the Bible* (Abingdon, 1977), Jesus proposed a solution to patriarchy's male dominance/female submission which is far more radical than Mary Daly's switching of divine roles. Jesus taught and enacted mutuality, in which greatness is demonstrated by voluntary servanthood and hence the empowerment of all those who are lacking in power. Many people experience difficulty trying to imagine how the model of mutuality would work out politically, asserting that it cannot work in a unit as small as the nuclear family, let alone in larger societal structures. "Somebody has to make the final decisions," runs the familiar argument. But I think that such arguments arise because the human imagination has been narrowed and strangulated by centuries of patriarchal practices and theories.

It is enough for me that Jesus insisted on mutuality and that he drew his illustrations from the political structures of his day. For instance, when his disciples were disputing about their relative greatness, Jesus said, "In the world, kings lord it over their subjects; and those in authority are called their country's 'Benefactors.' Not so with you: on the contrary, the highest among you must bear himself like the youngest, the chief of you like a servant" (Luke 22:25-26 NEB). I do not for one moment believe it to be beyond human ingenuity to devise and implement the details of a workable political system on the model of mutuality rather than dominance and submission. It would be a long process, very taxing, but it could be done. Jesus gave us the model two thousand years ago, but it was such a radical departure from patriarchy's world-image that not even the developing church structures implemented it. Nevertheless, the alternative image is there, ready to help us free ourselves from patriarchal snares. The prophetic vision has been given to us. To begin its implementation along feminist (human equality) lines is to *begin* to practice a Christian power structure, not to destroy it. It is impossible to destroy a structure that has never been implemented.

Despite all that, I have to face the fact that Jesus not only taught the political model of mutuality but also used and actively taught a God-language that has helped reinforce the patriarchal images of the Old Testament— the very images that have empowered the male imagination to identify with divinity. In fact, in one of the very passages where Jesus teaches the mutuality model, the God-language problem becomes particularly acute. It's Matthew 23:8-12 (NEB): "But you must not be called 'rabbi'; for you have one Rabbi, and you are all brothers. Do not call any man on earth 'father'; for you have one Father, and he is in heaven. Nor must you be called 'teacher'; you have one Teacher, the Messiah. The greatest among you must be your servant. For whoever exalts himself will be humbled; and whoever humbles himself will be exalted."

The mutuality model is certainly taught here. The only distinction to be maintained is the distinction between the Creator (the whole Pattern or Process of Reality) and the creature (*part* of the Pattern or Process of Reality). No isolated ego, no individual person, is to take upon herself or himself the final authoritativeness of the Totality, the Unifier of the Universe, God. In other words, it is basic to human wisdom to be able to distinguish the part from the Whole and to relate to all the other parts as members of one single Body, being "subject to one another out of reverence for Christ" (Eph. 5:21 NEB).

But, oh, that masculine language. "Father!" "Brothers!" Actually, English translations make the passage sound more "masculist" than it is. The Greek word *adelphoi*, translated *brothers or brethren,* actually means "of the same womb," "siblings," or "relatives." But still the word *patēr* makes the image distinctly male. Why did Jesus choose to reinforce patriarchal imagery rather than doing a *really* new thing? Why didn't he choose exclusively female God-images, or exclusively androgynous God-images? Why didn't he appoint female disciples? Why, for that matter, wasn't God incarnated as a woman? Then the oppressive trials of women would all have been ended.

Or would they? Suppose Jesus had used exclusively female imagery about God; then, Christianity might have become the religion that empowered female imaginations and weakened male ones. Inevitably it would have taken very little time for confusion to set in concerning the mother in heaven and Jesus' human

mother, so that "Maryolatry" would have been practiced
in a way no religion has ever practiced it, with all the
self-deprecating implications of one human being's total
adulation of another. And of course our political and
societal structures would have become as strongly
matriarchal as they currently are patriarchal. Would that
be any advantage to the human race as a whole? I don't
think so.

Suppose Jesus had used exclusively androgynous
God-imagery, teaching us to pray to "Our Father-
Mother who art in heaven." In the context of human
experience, the problem with androgyny is that it is an
imaginative construct *only*; so very few people could
willingly imagine such a Heavenly Being and identify
with it and thus feel empowered by it. The concept of
psychological androgyny has great usefulness, because it
focuses on the psyche rather than the body. I frequently
make use of the concept myself. But I am grateful that
Jesus did not ask me to imagine and pray to an
androgyne that has no visible human counterpart
outside a medical ward.

Suppose Jesus had used exclusively neuter images:
God as ground, or water, or wind, but never as male or
female. Then Christianity might have become imbued
with neopagan worship of the natural world. And there
would have been very little sense of comfort, of a God to
whom I could cry out "Abba!" (Daddy! or Mommy!). It's
not easy to cuddle up to the Ground of Being, and
although I perceive myself as fully adult, sometimes I do
want to imagine the Whole of which I am part as being
cuddly, nurturant, and protective.

But in fact Jesus spoke of God predominantly in
masculine images, occasionally in feminine images (for
instance, Luke 15:8-10, Luke 13:34, John 3:6), occa-

sionally in images drawn from nature (the vine, the wind, the living water), and also in role descriptions that are not sexually differentiated (the word, the way, the door, the shepherd). But male images predominate. Why?

One factor, of course, is Jesus' experience as a human being in a patriarchal culture. Here I am reminded of the vital importance of understanding any book as speaking primarily out of the time and place in which it was written, and of evaluating any person's career within the framework of where he or she is coming from. (How *different* my career would have been had I been born not into a fundamentalist family but into a liberal Christian home—or into a family of another religion, or no religion! Because I would have been shaped by and therefore reacting against different factors, everything that I might have said or written would have to be viewed from a different angle.) According to Philippians 2:5-8, Jesus' self-emptying of divine prerogatives was a deliberately chosen act. In order to model voluntary servanthood to a culture that was both sexist and slave-owning, Jesus had to have power; so the human form to be taken on had to be part of the power-group of that particular society. Hence, Jesus was born both male and free.

Jesus was modeling and preaching a radically different life-style. Not radically different from the one envisioned by the greatest prophets of the Old Testament, but radically different from the actualities of society at the time of his birth. To communicate at all, he had to use language people could comprehend. And anybody who has ever worked for social change knows that it is self-defeating to confront people too rapidly with too much that is new to them. The more startling the concepts, the more familiar should be the language in which they are couched.

Jesus was talking to people who were accustomed to thinking about God in almost exclusively masculine terms. Because he was trying to get across to them some radically different ideas about the ordering of society, he tried to modify the imagining process by occasionally speaking of God in nonmasculine images: as a woman seeking her lost coin, as a hen sheltering her chickens, or as the mother of all the twice-born. Most of the time, however, he accommodated his God-language to patterns his audience would feel more comfortable with.

As we saw in Matthew 23:8-12, Jesus utilized conventional God-language to teach a very *un*conventional use of power. Had his followers stuck to the pattern of mutual servanthood, which he not only *taught* but *lived* among his disciples (including the many women who traveled with him and supported him, Luke 8:2-3), there never would have developed the hierarchical church structures we Christians face today. Those empowered by the image of God as male would have used their power to empower women and to set free and empower their slaves.

The same sort of accommodation of language patterns occurs in the New Testament Epistles. Although Paul was teaching the mutual submission (concern, supportiveness, respect) of every Christian to every other Christian in Ephesians 5, utilizing the organic image of a head that depends upon its body and a body that depends upon its head, he did not say *outright* that Christian husbands should submit themselves to their wives just as the wives submitted themselves to their husbands. (Elsewhere, in I Corinthians 7:3-5, he did indicate sexual equality and mutuality by insisting that "the husband must give the wife what is due to her, and the wife equally must give the husband his due"— NEB.)

But in Ephesians 5:25 he instructed Christian husbands to follow the model of Christ's voluntary self-emptying of divine prerogatives ("love your wives, as Christ also loved the church and *gave himself up for it*" —NEB). Italics mine. Thus, he asked the first-century husband, holder of absolute power in the owner-property model of marriage, to introduce a truly Christian marital structure by forgoing ownership and becoming the servant of his wife. She could not have become the head or source of the Christian marital structure because she had no power of which to divest herself. But once the husband had become the head or source of mutuality by giving up his traditional male prerogatives and serving his wife, the wife was expected to respond by serving her husband in return. Thus Paul avoided outright statements of husbandly subjection-in-mutuality (which might have so stunned first-century minds that it would have confused the issue anyway) and yet presented a model of mutuality that much of even today's "Christian" society still refuses to heed.

It is centuries since the biblical vision of mutuality was offered to humankind. I think it is time that my own ways of thinking about God should build upon what the biblical authors gave me, despite their patriarchal era, bringing their concepts forward into terms meaningful for citizens of the twentieth century. I sense that a thorough overhaul of my own imaginative patterns will be part of my contribution to a more equitable society. And I hope that the church of the 1980s will put the "language issue" high on its priority list; for according to Romans 12:2, the way to be transformed is by the renewing of our *minds*.

8
Imaging God Inclusively

To begin on the task of imaging God inclusively, I could implement in my own thought-patterns the biblical insight that "God is spirit"—*not* by degrading body and elevating spirit, but rather by emphasizing the universal dimensions of the "spiritual body" of God-in-Christ. John 4:24 gives assistance in that direction, telling me that "God is spirit, and those who worship [God] must worship in spirit and in truth" (NEB). This statement offers the worship-experience to everybody because no one is cut off from access to *spirit*, to that which is intangible yet so real that we call the absence of it death and the presence of it life. Prison walls cannot cut a person off from spirit, nor can color, or poverty, or lack of education. It is true that tyrannical societies seek to *break the spirit* in order to render an individual thought-lessly obedient. But it is significant that God takes special care of people whose spirits have been broken: "I will seek that which was lost, and bring again that which was driven away, and will bind up that which was broken, and will strengthen that which was sick" (Ezek. 34:16 KJV).

It is the cumulative effect of female experience that warns me against using "God is spirit" in the traditional way of setting up a hierarchy, with spirit superior to body. For centuries, females have been associated with the body and its passions, while males have associated themselves with the mind and spirit, with reason. And the concomitant value-judgment has been, of course, that reason (good) must control passion (evil). From there it has been only a tiny step to the association of females with the demonic and males with the deity. Because so much has been written on this subject in recent years, I need not labor the point.

Most Christians are aware that biblical injunctions about living "in the spirit" rather than "in the flesh" are not aimed at defamation of the physical body, but rather are used to distinguish between locating one's ultimate identity in the private, localized ego-consciousness ("the flesh") as opposed to locating one's ultimate identity within the universal "spiritual body" shared with all created beings and amounting to more than the sum of its parts (the Body of Christ, "the spirit").

There is nothing bad about the physical body and nothing bad about the localized ego-consciousness, although from the biblical standpoint there is something *temporary* about both. The body that will be resurrected will apparently be qualitatively different, a "spiritual body," according to I Corinthians 15:44; but the fact that *body* is slated for resurrection says something about the goodness of body. And the consciousness that knows as it is known (I Cor. 12:12) is also qualitatively different from the severely limited temporal consciousness. It is only when my human ego *absolutizes itself* and the physical body it resides in that I am thrown into a state of alienation from God (the Wholeness of Being and Becoming) and hence from all other creatures. Inevitably at such times, I fear the death of my physical body and want my own advancement more than anybody else's.

Human divisiveness is based either upon egomaniacal parochialism (absolutizing my ideas and my methods) or upon bodily distinctions (whites treating blacks inhumanly on the assumption that black skin means inferiority; Nazis incinerating Jews because of their race and homosexuals because of their predilections; males dominating females because of differences in shape and musculature). All of this oppression is the result of idolatry, the worship of the creature (the severely limited, localized ego) rather than the Creator (present in all "spiritual bodies" everywhere).

But my point is that none of this represents assuming a "superior spirit" over an "inferior body"; rather, there is the *idolatrous* spirit-identified-with-localized-physical-body (called "worldly" in the New Testament) over against *worshipful* spirit-body-identified-with-universal-ized-Spirit-Body-of-New-Humanity (called "godly" in the New Testament). God is spirit. Spirit is incarnated (embodied) in New Humanity, of which Christ was the firstborn (Rom. 8:29). To worship God, I must be "in spirit" and "in truth"; that is, my whole being, body-soul-spirit, must be identified or in harmony with what is truly real, the New Humanity's Body-Soul-Spirit as pioneered by the resurrected Christ.

In the New Creation, there is no exclusion of any*body* on any basis whatsoever. According to Galatians 3:27-28, we all become one person, one body inside one garment (the Christ). For centuries, of course, representatives of the church have been speaking of the Messiah, the Christ, as God incarnated, spirit embodied, Word enfleshed, divinity humanized, humankind divinized. But not many have taken the next logical step of recognizing that if this is true, then it makes perfect sense to imagine the Christ as female, black, Indian, Oriental, poor Appalachian white, or indeed as *any form created beings can take.* (I think of Gerard Manley Hopkins' poem for whom Christ broke forth from the sight of a falcon riding on the wind—"The Windhover: To Christ Our Lord.")

The Christ is in no created form *exclusively,* but in all such forms *inclusively* ("in him all things hold together," Col. 1:17). For in the New Creation, "There is one body and one Spirit, . . . who is over all and through all and in all" (Eph. 4:4-6 NEB). This kind of imaging, based squarely upon an inclusive reading of Scripture, supports social justice, because it makes available to every human being the empowerment of identifying herself or himself with the divine. It also provides the best possible basis for restraint in the use of natural resources.

Second, I can learn to think of the word *God* as the designation of an office or role (the whole Structure and Process of Reality) rather than as a masculine word denoting a physical masculine person like Jove on Mount Olympus. The problem of imaging exclusively a Goddess or Great Mother is that it tends to fragment Reality in the same way that literalistic imaging of God as exclusively Father has done. Worse yet, because of centuries of patriarchal condescension toward women, *feminizing* a word immediately tends to *trivialize* it. Apart from a small contingent of feminist theologians, people feel that the role of deity is split and trivialized by feminizing the word used to designate it. The feminist theologians who prefer to speak only of the Goddess will, of course, object that that is exactly their point: the human consciousness must learn to recognize the female as equally as divine as the male. With that point I fully agree; but I doubt that designating the office of deity as Goddess is the way to go about it. Let me make some analogies to illustrate.

The moment one speaks of a *chairwoman,* because of social conditioning the imagination pictures garden clubs and theater parties. The word *chairperson* was invented to allow both males and females to imagine themselves in such leadership roles. But in actual practice *chairperson* has not been used when men chaired (they remained chairmen) but only when women were chairing. The end result was not an advance for women, but a wipeout of our bodily nature, our femaleness. *Chairperson* has therefore only made matters worse. The solution would be either to use the neutral word *chair* as a noun as well as a verb, or to view the word *chairman* as a designation of office or role rather than as sexually differentiated. In this case I think the word *chair* is clearly the more satisfactory solution. It focuses on work to be done (chairing) without designating the sex of the doer.

Alma Graham has written of the "language of equal opportunity," arguing that women are invariably trivialized when jobs are labeled as if work varied according to the sex of the worker. Reading Graham's article, I recalled that Katharine Hepburn, who has a powerful self-concept, has always referred to herself as an actor; she is "one who acts on the stage or screen." By analogy, a woman who writes books is an author, not an authoress; a woman who executes a will is an executor, not an executrix; a woman who is elected to the highest post in her government is a president, not (God forbid!) a presidentrix or a presidentress. Jobs should properly be named by the work performed, irrespective of the sex of the performer. So I should train myself to think of an insurance *agent* rather than an insurance man, a telephone line *repairer*, an oil *deliverer*, a mail *carrier*, a *member* of Congress. Such language makes it possible for anyone to make imaginative identification with any job and thus to be empowered to seek it.

If, then, society learns to think about the word *God* not as the name of a specific person (analogous to Jove) but rather as a job description or the designation of an office—the only office that contains no external limitations, and certainly not the limitation of human sexuality—then we will have opened up that concept to every human being. The fact that the Bible uses the word *God* for the One Deity and the same word for pagan idols (uncapitalized) seems to indicate that the word is to be thought of as designating an office (Supreme Being) rather than a proper name. And the fact that both male and female are made in God's image and designated as God's agents (Gen. 1:26-27) ought to help demolish the notion that the term *God* is sex-defined (or confined).

In this connection, I am reminded of my reaction when first I read the anonymous medieval work called *The Cloud of Unknowing.* The edition I used was the Doubleday paperback edited by William Johnston, which includes also *The Book of Privy Counselling* by the same unidentified mystic. Having been reared on strictly propositional Christianity, I was astounded to be told in *Privy Counselling*: "When you go apart to be alone for prayer . . . reject all thoughts, be they good or be they evil. See that nothing remains in your conscious mind save a naked intent stretching out towards God. Leave it stripped of every particular idea about God . . . " (p. 149). I realized, with a jolt, that even my ideas about God are part of my ego-consciousness, part of the knowledge which will vanish away, part of my private judgment-system which must be *relinquished* if I am to enjoy real communion with the divine.

I read on. My fourteenth-century mentor, whoever she or he may be, counseled me that "I want your thought of self to be as naked and simple as your thought of God, so that you may be spiritually united to him without any fragmentation and scattering of your mind. He is your being and in him, you are what you are, not only because he is the cause and being of all that exists, but because he is *your* cause and the deep center of *your* being. Therefore . . . think of yourself and him in the same way: that is with the simple awareness that he is as he is, and that you are as you are. In this way your thought will not be fragmented or scattered, but unified in him who is all" (p. 150). I feel no doubt that were that medieval mystic living today, those masculine pronouns concerning God would instantly be either expanded or deleted. Clearly the author thinks of *God* as the designation of an all-inclusive Presence beyond any human *comprehension,* let alone any human *limitation.* As I encountered these great insights, I realized how very grateful I felt to the Women's Movement for forcing me out of the mold of thinking of God as somehow definable according to human categories. And for that reason, a switch to Goddess-language is for me only a return to a mind-forged manacle, not liberation at all.

But I do consider it essential to be a witness to my belief that the word *God* designates an office and not a male being. To do this I must consistently use inclusive pronouns or at least avoid male pronouns. I prefer to repeat the term *God* rather than to use a limiting and therefore misleading masculine or feminine or neuter pronoun. This gets especially sticky when I need to use a reflexive construction. I could try James F. White's solution ("God gave Godself"), which is certainly better than "God gave himself." Or I could say "God gave herself/himself/itself" as an awkward but insistent way of driving home the absolute *inclusiveness* of the Godhead.

The thesis of *The Cloud of Unknowing* is that as long as I am living within the limitations of mortality, God will remain surrounded by a cloud of unknowing that I can in no way penetrate cognitively, but only by love. This realization is, the author assures me, truly liberating: "For in the realm of the spirit heaven is as near up as it is down, behind as before, to left or to right. The access to heaven is through desire. . . . We need not strain our spirit in all directions to reach heaven, for we dwell there already through love and desire" (p. 127). Although we twentieth-century people may flatter ourselves that through the scientific world-view we have liberated ourselves from naïve understanding of the universe and of a God-out-there, this fourteenth-century person understood *plenty*! And she or he would probably feel sorry for us as we flounder around struggling with God-language in almost primitive naïveté about the nature of worshiping "in spirit and in truth."

Third, I can stimulate more inclusive imaging of God by using a variety of biblically based epithets or ascriptions. In Old English poetry, word pictures were drawn by use of compound epithets called *kennings,* so that the ocean might be spoken of as the "whale-path," a king as a "ring-giver," or a sword as a "fire-flasher." Use of kenning-like epithets concerning God would serve as reminders of God's *myriad* roles in my life. Continual, repetitive reference to God as Mother or Father focuses attention on beginnings, on God's "creatorial" and parental functions only. (Even so, sometimes referring to God as Parent rather than as either Mother or Father forces me to think about *what parenting is* apart from sex roles: what is its *essence?*) But constant searching for fresh biblical metaphors would widen my awareness of what God does not only *over,* but also *through* and *in* the creation: Sea-walker, Light-bringer, Sin-forgiver, Star-kindler, Whirlwind-speaker, Life-restorer.

Prayers may address God simply as "you," but when that feels too abrupt or my heart is overflowing with love, all sorts of phrases may grow out of scriptural usage such as, "you who have healing in your wings," "you who inhabit eternity," "you who are my rock," "you who swing the stars in space." And they may, of course, also be based on my own experience: "you who are my shield from gossip," "you who visit me on golden eyelids," "you who have provided the love of friends." None of this denies the importance of single-word ascriptions, such as, Redeemer, Sustainer, Friend, Comforter, or Guide.

Since all language about God is figurative and limited and probably to some degree a distortion of the One hidden within the "Cloud of Unknowing," I need constant reminders that no single phrase or word picture can possibly be telling the whole truth about God. Getting in a rut of a few too-narrow images tempts any person or group to forget that we do not yet know as we are known. From such forgetfulness springs idolatry, the absolutizing of our own minds and their imagery.

Fourth, I can help myself image God more inclusively by continuing to explore the female imagery occasionally applied to God in the Old and New Testaments. Although I included many such images in *Women, Men & the Bible* and added some more in the cassette study course by the same title, once in a while I come upon new ones. For instance, it excites me that when Jesus spoke to his disciples about the future time when they would have to do without his physical presence in the world, he described his own suffering and the history of suffering humanity through a birth-metaphor: "When a woman is in travail she has sorrow, because her hour has come; but when she is delivered of the child, she no longer remembers the anguish, for joy that a child is born into the world" (John 16:21 RSV). A few minutes later, John tells us, Jesus began his prayer with the words, "The hour has come." Thus he identified the anguish of the cross with the pangs of giving birth, and identified himself with a woman in labor. His pain would be forgotten as soon as he had given birth to the New Humanity.

One reason this image excites me is that this very passage was part of my personal oppression. When it was time for me to go into the hospital to give birth to Paul, my gynecologist, a professing Christian, quoted to me what he probably still quotes to every woman as she goes into labor: "A woman when she is in travail hath sorrow, because her hour is come: but as soon as she is delivered of the child, she remembereth no more the anguish, for joy that *a man* is born into the world" (KJV). Italics mine. Because he had told me that my child would be a girl, my heart wrenched when I heard the reference to a man-child. As a new contraction started, I groaned, "But what if it's a girl?" He shrugged, "Oh, I don't imagine the sex of the baby matters much to God." Nevertheless, I was triumphant when I had a boy, partly because, unconsciously, I was convinced that John 16:21 really implied that boys were better than girls. To the detriment of my self-respect, I continued to think so for many years. No wonder: not only the King James

Version, but also contemporary versions such as the New English Bible, the Phillips New Testament in Modern English, and The Jerusalem Bible all speak of the joy of a *man's* birth. Yet the Greek Word *anthropos* translated "a man" clearly means "a human being"—not a male person, but simply a person. In such ways has female presence and power in Scripture—and in the imagination of religious women—been nearly eradicated.

As biblical feminists keep coming up with new awareness of the female aspects of the Godhead, I think several cautions are in order. One of them is that I doubt the wisdom of referring to the Holy Spirit as the feminine Person of the Holy Trinity. Such separation breaks the unity of the One Godhead, as if there were really three gods in Christianity, two of them male and one of them female. Besides, such separation still leaves the female in the minority, eternally "outvoted" by a two-to-one power bloc, and therefore does very little for the female self-concept. In addition, the Bible utilizes female imagery in connection with all three Persons of the Trinity, and I believe it is best to mirror scriptural usage as much as possible. However, because we are engaged in struggling out of the shackles of patriarchy, we will want to increase the *proportion* of female imagery concerning the Godhead; and of course we will want to take special pains to affirm the right of all human beings to imagine God in the ways that empower them as blacks or Indians or Orientals or whatever.

My second caution is that we must not imagine that the use of feminine imagery concerning the Godhead will be enough by itself to bring about an end of sexist oppression in society or even in the church community. Unless the "feminine" roles and aspects of God are *valued* as highly as the "masculine" roles and aspects, our sense that "the Lord our God is one" will still be fragmented, males will still be encouraged toward primacy, women will still be diminished into secondary status, and community will still be broken. My favorite illustration of this comes from one of the sermons of the great English poet and preacher, John Donne. Because he was a careful student of the Bible, Donne occasionally spoke of God in feminine terms; but he regarded God-as-Mother as distinctly more "infirm" and unquestionably "inferior" to God-as-Father. Consequently, at a wedding he felt free to speak of the woman as the man's "staff," commenting that, after all, nobody values his staff as much as he does his own legs. It would be hard to imagine a more flagrant violation of the injunction in Ephesians 5 for husbands to love their wives *as their own bodies*"; but Donne and his congregation were reading the Bible through sexist-colored glasses.

As long as people continue to value spirit more than body, then images of God feeding her children will be preempted in Christian imaginations by male priests in flowing gowns handing out bread and wine and washing the dishes afterward upon the altar. And males will continue guarding their male province of spiritual food from women, who will be encouraged to stick to the more humble job of handing out food to physical bodies and washing the dishes afterward in the kitchen. So whereas I in no way retract what I said earlier about the political power of the imagination, I want to point out that the process can work in the other direction as well. Changes in societal structures will help our imaginations become more inclusive and empowering. When fathers share fully in parenting tasks and mothers share fully in spiritual leadership, we will all be in a better position to image God more expansively.

9
Interiority And Ecumenism

Some years ago a friend told me about a place called Pacem in Terris, in Warwick, New York, about twenty minutes from my home in Upper Greenwood Lake, New Jersey. Best described as a "place of inwardness," Pacem in Terris is a chapel constructed by artist Frederick Franck out of the ruins of an old mill. The chapel is transreligious in the sense that no symbol is exclusive to any one religion. The fish, candles, wheat, grapes, rock, water, wood, human faces—all the symbols and materials have a universal resonance. If anyone feels excluded at Pacem in Terris, it is probably because the inwardness and all-inclusiveness of its orientation feel somehow threatening to the narrower religious tradition many people are comfortable with.

At Pacem in Terris, Frederick and Claske Franck sponsor plays, workshops, poetry readings, and concerts, all of them geared toward meditation rather than toward showiness. Not long after I began to frequent the Sunday afternoon programs, there was a production of Frederick Franck's re-creation of the medieval play of *Everyman*. Since both my son Paul and my friend Lynne Pattin were part of the cast, I went to see the play repeatedly. It has recently been published by Doubleday under the title *EveryOne: The Timeless Myth of "Everyman" Reborn* (1978).

Although there is no substitute for experiencing the play for oneself, either in performance or in its printed form, perhaps a quotation from it will help to illustrate both the tremendous debt I owe to the Francks and the ways my understanding seems to differ from theirs. At the end of the play, the voice of God speaks:

. . . I am the One,
I am the Many
I am in All
You touch, you see,

I AM
THE STRUCTURE
OF
REALITY.

Stop chattering about Me!
About my Son . . .
Who is my Son
but he who dares
to see Me,
dares embrace Me,
RELENTLESS
STRUCTURE OF REALITY.

He is my Son
whose living flesh
reveals My image,
SHOWS
WHAT IS DIVINE

IN MAN,
Who dies
but knows no death,

who brings
MY HEALING SPIRIT,
that makes all One,
that makes One All,
MY HOLY SPIRIT.

Eternally mocked
and spat at is my Son,
Eternally betrayed,
starved,
tortured,
gassed,
murdered
is my Son.

ETERNALLY
I RESURRECT HIM
DEEP
IN THE
HUMAN CORE!

Despite the masculine language, I am reassured of the inclusive intentions of the author not only by the concepts themselves but also by the fact that the role of God is usually played by a woman. (Sometimes a woman is also cast in the starring role, that of EveryOne.) Perhaps it was repeatedly hearing the voice of God represented by Claske Berndes Franck's rich female voice, speaking English with her delicious Dutch accent, which first enabled me to dare to begin an imaginative connection with God as reflected in my dream life and in my subsequent thinking.

When first Pacem in Terris became part of my life, I was bewildered by some of the sayings that were foreign to my upbringing. In particular I was bewildered by the transparent eye that is set in the wall of the chapel and inscribed with Meister Eckhart's famous remark, "The eye with which I see God is the same eye with which God sees me." I have since discovered the meaning of that remark by reading not only Eckhart himself but also many other Eastern and Western spiritual classics as well as many of the books of Frederick Franck. Among the latter, I found *Pilgrimage to Now/Here* (Orbis Press, 1974) to be especially enlightening.

Ultimately, however, it was through my own experience that I learned what Eckhart was talking about—especially the "experience of the golden eyelids" described earlier. The interior journey can be read about and talked about, but like all the most essential experiences in life, it is not understood until it has been *lived*. Even then it is not fully understood, for it is foolishness to think that what is begotten, born, and dies (physically) can ever fully encompass what Dr. Franck refers to as "the nameless Name."

At first I was extremely resistant to the idea that God

could in any way be identified with the depths of my own being. The idea seemed to me to be antithetical to biblical concepts. When I read somewhere that the Bible stated that through Christ we human beings were intended to become "partakers of the divine nature," I made a dash for my concordance, unable to believe that such a stunning statement could be in the Bible yet never have been mentioned in all my years of four church services a week. Yet there it was, big as life, in II Peter 1:4. Furthermore, I found reference to it in such bastions of orthodoxy as Calvin's *Institutes of the Christian Religion*. And I began to discover one biblical passage after another that teaches the absolute identification of God with humanity through Christ: "He that is joined unto the Lord is one spirit" (I Cor. 6:17 KJV); "Christ liveth in me" (Gal. 2:20 KJV); "Christ is all, and in all" (Col. 3:11 KJV); Christ "filleth all in all" (Eph. 1:23 KJV); and many more. I had sometimes heard commentary on these passages, but Christ's presence within me had always been described as a take-over by Someone Totally Other, as if a pacemaker had been installed in my chest to control my behavior. There is an enormous difference between the installation of a foreign object within human nature and the organic identification of human nature with the divine Being. Slowly it dawned upon me that Jesus' own expressions were of *organic* oneness: the vine and the branches, the internal fountain of living water, interrelating within the Godhead extended to include humankind (John 17), and so forth.

I also discovered that Eckhart was not alone in identifying his own inner eye with the eye of God. Centuries before Eckhart, St. Athanasius had articulated a similar principle: Christ, he said, "became man so that we might be made God." St. Augustine recorded in his

Confessions that the voice of God told him, "Grow, and then thou shalt feed on Me. Nor shalt thou change Me into thy substance as thou changest the food of thy flesh, but thou shalt be changed into Mine." As Evelyn Underhill pointed out, Eckhart was simply expanding the view of the church fathers when he wrote "Our Lord says to every living soul, 'I became man for you. If you do not become God for me, you do me wrong.' " (Incidentally, Underhill's book entitled *Mysticism,* first published in 1911 and currently available in Dutton paperback, remains the best general introduction to the nature and development of spiritual consciousness. It would be impossible to overstate my enthusiasm for that book.)

I have been encouraged by the discovery of a remarkable consensus of opinion stretching across centuries of people who have made the inward journey. In Rabbi Abraham Isaac Kook (1865–1935) I found substantial agreement with the experience of Christian mystics: "The primary role of penitence . . . " writes the rabbi, "is for the person to return to himself, to the root of his soul. Then, he will at once return to God, to the Soul of all souls" (*The Lights of Penitence,* Paulist Press edition, p. 117). In Lao-tzu, a Chinese poet of the sixth century B.C., I found a similar insight: "Empty yourself of everything. / Let the mind rest at peace. / The ten thousand things rise and fall while the Self watches their return. / They grow and flourish and then return to the source. / . . . Being divine, you will be at one with the Tao. / Being at one with the Tao is eternal. / And though the body dies, the Tao will never pass away" (*Tao Te Ching,* translated by Gia Fu Feng and Jane English, Vintage Books, 1972).

A special surprise was in store for me when I

discovered similar insights in the work of a contemporary evangelical and ex-missionary, Norman Grubb. He writes: "There is really only One Person in the universe, and that is God. . . . Everything is a form of God, a manifestation of God. The visible is made out of the Invisible, as Hebrews 11:3 says. . . . We must bridge that gap of illusory separation. . . . Wherever we see things, we see [God] in one form or another. . . . God . . . is the All in us" (pp. 11-21, passim, *God Unlimited in Daily Living*, available from the Christian Literature Crusade, Fort Washington, Pennsylvania). Later I became aware of the Union Life ministry based in Glen Ellyn, Illinois, publishers of *Union Life* magazine, which is distinctly evangelical, yet sees God in everything and everybody.

While it would be impossible to bring about doctrinal agreement between people as diverse as Meister Eckhart, Evelyn Underhill, Lao-tzu, Frederick Franck, Rabbi Kook, and Norman Grubb, their words reveal a core of experience in which such people could find fellowship. I think there is an important lesson here for anyone interested in implementing the ecumenical vision of Ephesians 1:10, that God's goal for the fullness of time is "to unite all things" in Christ, who made possible and who embodies the New Humanity. That lesson is this: syncretism—the attempt to hammer out doctrinal, propositional agreement among people of various religions—is doomed to failure. But profound harmony is possible if people will cease quarreling about external forms and concentrate on the internal experience of entering into union with the nameless Name who is hidden within the Cloud of Unknowing, and then concentrate on expressing that union by serving humanity.

Through a fine book by Frithjof Schuon, *The Transcendent Unity of Religions,* I was helped to understand that when it comes to the interior journey—when it comes to the actual experience of union with the divine nature—the important distinction is between what is transcendent and eternal on the one hand, and what is temporal on the other. All doctrinal statements are human formulations and therefore are part of the knowledge that will pass away (I Cor. 13:8-10). What I call the Christ-nature, a Zen Buddhist would call the Buddha-nature, Rabbi Kook would call "the Soul of all souls," and Lao-tzu would call the Tao; but we all would be speaking of an experienced Truth that undergirds all religious forms whatsoever.

Although the Bible convinces me that redemption is made possible only through Christ, the Bible also convinces me that my understandings are only temporal, whereas people are eternal. Therefore, I would prefer to live harmoniously with people in whom the Holy Spirit has worked in different ways rather than to alienate myself from them because they refer to the nameless Name under terms different from my own. The Wind constantly breaches external forms; "so is every one that is born of the Spirit" (John 3:8b KJV).

Some people feel it necessary to hammer away at other people, trying to force them into conformity with their own way of seeing things—a divisive activity at best, brutally cruel at worst. Others try to compromise their belief-systems until they can discover a common doctrinal basis acceptable to everybody, but since ideas and rituals are external and hence clung to by the human ego, this is an attempt to gain unity on the level of the letter that kills rather than of the spirit that gives life. Only at the level where ego-judgments are relinquished, and the

Cloud of Unknowing is entered in desire and love for the divine, can the ecumenical experience bring unity to humankind.

In *The Last Battle* (Macmillan, 1956) C. S. Lewis tells the story of Emeth, who has spent his life sincerely serving a false god named Tash and who dies yearning to see Tash face to face. The name of Aslan, the great Lion who represents the one true God in the tales of Narnia, has always been hateful to Emeth. Scornfully Emeth rejects the syncretism that tries to blend Tash and Aslan into one single being called Tashlan. He is totally committed to Tash; so that when after death he sees Aslan and knows instantly that the Lion is "worthy of all honor," Emeth expects to be struck spiritually dead for his honest admission that he has always been a servant of Tash. He is amazed when the Lion tells him, "All the service thou hast done to Tash, I account as service done to me." Emeth asks whether the syncretists were right after all: is is true, then, that the Lion and Tash are one? But the Lion replies: "I and he are of such different kinds that no service which is vile can be done to me, and none which is not vile can be done to him. Therefore if any man swear by Tash and keep his oath for the oath's sake, it is by me that he has truly sworn, though he know it not, and it is I who reward him. And if any man do a cruelty in my name, then, though he says the name Aslan, it is Tash whom he serves and by Tash his deed is accepted" (p. 156).

According to the vision of Matthew 25:31-46, C. S. Lewis is correct. Assistance to the least prestigious of human beings is assistance to Christ; refusal to help needy human beings is refusal to help Christ. Whether the person who gives assistance thinks the assistance is given in the name of Christ or the Buddha or the Tao or

Allah or Jehovah or Tash, the assistance is given to Christ. I, therefore, can recognize my true sisters and brothers more surely by the way they live their lives than by the name they utter. I will not claw at those in whom I see the Spirit, trying to force them into doctrinal conformity with me. Neither will I cast aside those Christian concepts and symbols that are so dear to me. Retaining my loyalty to Jesus, I will simply enjoy communion with all those who manifest the fruits of the Spirit, even when we do not agree about external religious forms. Those who live in love live in God, and God in them (I John 4:16). And that's enough for me.

PART THREE: ACTION

10
Co-creating the New World

In the beginning, when God began to create, there was silence. Into that silence, God spoke the Word. Speech out of silence. And *action* out of speech: God spoke, and it was done. It is still that way. If I can silence my inner ego-babble long enough to listen, within my silence God speaks. And if my experience is an accurate index, within any centered and receptive spirit God will usually make clear what is the next authentic thing to say and do. There is and always has been a dynamic unity between speech, silence, and action that mirrors the dynamic triunity of the nature of Reality, the nature of God. I have come to understand that it is up to me to see to it that such dynamic triunity characterizes my life-experience.

I have been reinforced in that conviction by the song of the servant of Jehovah recorded in Isaiah 42 and 43:

"Thus says the Lord, / your Redeemer. / Behold, I am doing a new thing; / now it springs forth, do you not perceive it?" (43:14a, 19a RSV). The context indicates that the "new thing" is the bringing about of justice on the earth: "Behold my servant, whom I uphold, / my chosen, in whom my soul delights; / I have put my Spirit upon him, / he will bring forth justice to the nations. / . . . He will faithfully bring forth justice. / He will not fail or be discouraged till he has established justice in the earth" (42:1-4a).

I ask myself, "Is God still in the process of doing a new thing upon the earth?" And from my observation of what is happening in liberation movements all over the world, I think the answer is *yes*. Not only that, but from within comes the clarion conviction that I, like every other person born of the Spirit, am intended to be a co-creator, an incarnation of the continuing divine motion toward the New Creation that is currently springing forth. The sign of the Holy Spirit upon me will be just what Isaiah foretold: because I seek to be part of what Christ is doing in the cosmos, I am part of a Body that will not fail or be discouraged till we have "established justice in the earth." I do not deny that there may be other signs of the Holy Spirit's presence, such as speaking in tongues; but I seriously doubt that where active concern for establishing justice is absent, the Holy Spirit could be truly present.

Many centuries have gone by since Isaiah foretold the justice-process that would always involve the chosen servants of God, and until this date the justice that is in heaven has certainly not been fulfilled here on earth. But we can continue to work and pray for justice in the knowledge that the future we work for is a "previous future." I like that phrase because it depicts a future already completed in the all-encompassing present tense of God's Dynamic Being. It provides us with a certainty, a hope, and a promise that the play we are performing is a Divine *Comedy*.

But how, I ask myself, will the tragedy I perceive around me be transformed into a comedy of joy? I turn again to the Bible, seeking indications there concerning the teachings of Jesus and the accounts of what happened when people implemented those teachings. For instance, I turn to what was written to the believers at Ephesus: "Remember that at one time you Gentiles . . . were . . . separated from Christ. . . . But now in Christ Jesus you who once were far off have been brought near in the blood of Christ. For he is our peace, who has made us both one, and has broken down the dividing wall of hostility . . . that he might create in himself one new [person] in place of the two, so making peace, and might reconcile us both in God in one body through the cross, thereby bringing the hostility to an end" (2:11-16). Reading this, I remind myself that Ephesians was written from the vantage point of Paul the apostle, a Jew with an excellent family background and education. The book was addressed to people who had been converted to Christ not out of Judaism but out of paganism. Although many converts from Judaism in the early church looked down on converts from paganism because their families were not blessed by circumcision (the sign of God's covenant with Abraham), Ephesians does not capitalize on Paul's rank as one of the foremost of the Jewish converts.

Instead, the Epistle insists that the meaning of Christ's cross is the breaking down of that most basic wall of hostility in the early Christian church: the wall between Jewish and Gentile converts. This fact leads me to believe that the reign of God on earth will come only by the continued and constant breaking down of the walls of hostility that we human beings erect against one another. I believe God is still trying, through the process of redemption, to make "one new person" in place of the myriads of human categories and miserable hierarchies. It is my job, and the job of the twice-born everywhere, to work as co-redeemers in the process of "bringing the hostility to an end."

Recently, after hearing a talk about the human function as "the hands of God" in establishing justice on the earth, an earnest young woman asked me, "Now that I know my responsibility, what do I *do* about it?" I recognized what she must have been feeling, for I have felt it myself. My answer was, of course, related to the whole interrelationship between speech, silence, and action that is the theme of this book. In the speech (get ready) stage, I must inform myself of the injustices that exist. (Ignorance is no excuse.) In the silence (get set) stage, I must ask God to clarify within me my own authentic agenda for action. Since no one person can do everything, I must get my priorities straight within a peaceful, unhurried center, aware that others in God's community are empowered to do what I cannot do. And then it's time to get involved, to act, to *go*.

Obviously, there is nothing I can tell those who listen to me or read my work about what action is authentic to *them*. I can only talk about those actions authentic for me, in the hope that my process may be helpful to someone else.

Most recently, I have been involved in expanding my vision to make it more truly global. The first step, of course, has been attempting to inform myself and make real to myself the enormous inequities in the world.

For instance, I was jarred when I ran across a statement by Julius Nyerere, President of Tanzania, to the effect that instead of being one, the world is more divided than ever before—between the minority who *have* and the majority who *lack*, the minority who dominate and the majority who are dominated, the minority who exploit and the majority who are exploited. I was particularly struck by his comment that the well-fed minority has white skin and has adopted the Christian religion. In the first place, I am not used to thinking of myself as a member of the *oppressing* minority. In the second place, I am not used to thinking about the white race as a *minority*—but of course it is very much a minority in the world context. A sobering thought occurs to me: what if this white minority race I belong to should be treated by the majority the same way we whites have treated blacks, Indians, Orientals, and other "outsiders" for centuries?

In *The Radical Bible* (Orbis, 1972) I ran across an illustration that gave further assistance in making human injustice and need *real* to me. (I cannot understand astronomically large figures and statistics. I need things boiled down to numbers I can grasp.) I was asked to imagine that the whole human race alive today—over three billion people—is a village of just one thousand persons. In that village of one thousand, only 164 persons could be classified as living a moderately comfortable life. The other 836 persons are living lives of desperation and degradation. They are poor, diseased, economically oppressed, sexually oppressed, and politically oppressed. These were numbers I could readily picture, and they made me very uneasy, because I know that Ephesians 3:15 instructs me to remember that every family in heaven and earth is named after one single divine Parent and that in Christ Jesus those whom I have regarded as *They* are brought into complete and utter identification with me and mine, with *Us*. We all become one Body, one person, "partakers of the promise in Christ Jesus" (Eph. 3:6).

I know what I would do if I were not among the 164 persons who are living moderately comfortable lives in the global village of one thousand. Provided my spirit were not totally crushed, I would try with everything in me to overcome the barrier of injustice and achieve a more equitable distribution of resources. But if I obey the insight of Ephesians 3 and of many other New Testament passages that tell me the human race is a single organism because of creation and redemption, then I am forced to recognize that in the eyes of Love (God) I already *am* one with the 836 others in the global village who are living under conditions of agonizing poverty and oppression. My responsibility toward them is a responsibility toward my own family and my own self.

I cannot evade my global responsibility by telling myself that as a Christian, I have to be concerned only for those oppressed persons who are confessing members of the Christian religion. I cannot do that because according to Scripture, it is the will of God to "unite *all* things in [Christ], things in heaven and things on earth" (Eph. 1:10). Italics mine. Since the goal is the total uniting of the entire creation within the divine/human being of Christ Jesus, "being rooted and grounded in Christ's love" means that I must learn to see *every* person as *in Christ,* identified with Christ.

Although I am not by nature and socialization a very political person, an honest reading of Ephesians 1:10 forces me to see that God's goal is the uniting of all *things* in heaven and earth. All *things*, I must concede, would include not only the whole human creation, but the whole animal world, the whole vegetable and mineral world, and—here's the hardest part for me—all the societal structures, such as national government; business, religious, and military hierarchies; and even multinational corporations. Although my early religious training emphasized the importance of decency only in interpersonal relationships, I am forced to recognize that I have a political responsibility extending far beyond the private sphere of life. But between my female socialization and the concept of salvation as a purely private contract with God, I have had and still have a great deal of inertia to overcome.

For instance, I had always assumed that when Jesus said to Pilate, "My kingdom is not of this world," he meant that the kingdom of God is a purely spiritual matter having nothing to do with the unjust social structures of this world. I therefore found it easy to believe what I was taught, that Christian churches properly have no business getting involved in politics and social reform. But I have come to see that Jesus was not telling Pilate that his kingdom was otherworldly in the sense that it was unrelated to the inequities of a fallen world. Rather, Jesus was telling Pilate that his kingdom had nothing to do with national egotism, or with the racial, religious, ethnic, economic, and sexist ego-interests that pit human beings against one another. Jesus was saying: "I am the King of the Jews, all right, but not in the narrow worldly way *you* would define as being King of the Jews. Not in the sense of King of the *Jews* as a nation pitted against the Roman nation and oppressed by the Roman nation. My kingdom is not of this world because it is a kingdom where there is *no oppression at all*—no dominance, no enforced submission, no inequity, no division, no walls of hostility. My kingdom is not of this world, because it is a kingdom in which all the 'others,' all the outcasts, all the poverty-stricken, all the 'Gentiles,' all the people considered to be secondary, become fellow heirs, members of the same body, and partakers of God's promise."

The writings of William Stringfellow, Richard Mouw, and others have helped me understand that when the author of Ephesians urges me to fight against "the principalities, against the powers, against the world rulers of this present darkness, against the spiritual hosts of wickedness in the heavenly places" (6:12), the battle is more than a struggle for personal purity. The principalities and powers I am to struggle against include many basic assumptions of the American military machine, the Houses of Congress, and the huge corporations whose selfish interests control so much international policy. In short, I have become convinced that it is the job of believers, both as individuals and as church bodies, to let our contemporary powers know about the fact that God views the whole family of humankind as a single entity; that injustices done to any segment of humanity are injustices against the person of Christ and therefore are injustices against us all.

This conviction forces upon me another realization: when Christian churches and individual church members (myself, for instance) remain silent in the face of this world's enormous inequities, we place ourselves in heresy. When we assume that whatever our government does to other nations must be all right because it is *Us* against *Them*, we are guilty of national egotism, which is a form of idolatry. When we forget that *everyone else in the world is equally precious to God as we are to ourselves,* we are guilty of personal egotism, which is also idolatry. (I pon-

dered that at 5:30 one morning while I was anxiously
waiting my turn in a gas line behind seventy-two other
cars.) When in American homes people still assume that
the male's career is necessarily primary while the female's
is secondary and supportive, that assumption is a denial
of mutual servanthood that desensitizes children to the
oneness and universality of Christ's Body. I have
preached that truth, but I still struggle with my own old
nature to act out fully my theoretical awareness that
when I see *anyone* else as secondary to myself for *any*
reason, I deny what the New Testament insists upon, that
all of us are members of the same Body.

I know from Scripture that God's promise to bless all
nations is as infinite as the breadth and height and length
and depth of the love of Christ. But I have also
experienced the fact that I can limit the effects of the
promise for myself through a failure of perception.
While I am perceiving my oneness with the whole human
family, my efforts on behalf of others reward me with the
assurance of God's loving presence at the center of my
being. But when I succumb to egocentricity and feel
unconcerned about selfishness in myself and society, I
deny my membership in Christ's Body and feel cut off
from the love of Christ. (I am not *in fact* cut off, but my
own myopic attitude at those moments makes me *feel* cut
off.)

Out of these experiences I have realized that if the
structures of the Christian churches refuse to work
actively to establish justice in this world, then they are
refusing to cooperate with the plan of God, which is
through the church to make known the oneness of God's
human family to the principalities and powers (Eph.
3:10). Many of America's churches have become tools
and mirrors of the status quo, legitimizing the injustice

of American society, providing rationalizations for the
rich instead of empowerment for the poor. Such church
structures are among the principalities and powers that I
must war *against,* since they exclude from their leadership and concern those persons who are poor, nonwhite,
female, gay, or otherwise second class.

Because of my background, at first it seemed to me
inflated to think of myself as an embodiment of God in
the world. I was helped out of that fear-pattern by
attention to many biblical passages, perhaps most notably
by a comparison between the way terms are used in the
Epistles of Colossians and Ephesians. For instance, the
Greek word translated *economy* or *plan* is used in
Colossians 1:25 to mean a task or stewardship assigned to
a human being, whereas in Ephesians 3:9 the same word
is used to mean God's purpose for the consummation of
world history. At first glance this may look like a
contradiction. But the point in Ephesians is that by acting
upon human oneness within God's Spirit and because of
God's Spirit within me, I am "filled with all the fulness of
God." Therefore, what I as a human being do in striving
against injustice is actually the divine plan working itself
out through my stewardship of my time, energy, and
resources.

I also noticed that the word *mystery,* which in the
Pauline Epistles means "a revealed secret," is defined in
Colossians as "Christ in you, the hope of glory," but is
defined in Ephesians as uniting all things in Christ and
specifically as reconciling the Jewish converts with the
gentile ones. Here again, I realized, there is no
discrepancy, only a wonderful connection. Whereas
Colossians stresses the *personal aspect* of the mystery, that
Christ is in those who believe (therefore, in me!),
Ephesians stresses the *political effects* and ultimately the

cosmic effects of dying to egocentricity and living in the New Nature. Similarly with the definition of God's economy or plan: whereas Colossians stresses the personal aspect of God's assigning a task to a human steward, Ephesians stresses the cosmic results of God's cooperation with human agents. Such studies have encouraged me to believe that God really is the power at work within me, who can do far more abundantly than all that I ask or think (Eph. 3:20).

11
Taking Strides Toward Wholeness

Readings in Zen Buddhist and other oriental writings as well as the classics of Christian and Jewish mysticism have convinced me of humanity's general enslavement to a dualistic mode of thinking. Such dualism has alienated and fragmented us so drastically that it is hard even to think about wholeness, let alone experience it. Although philosophers might trace modern dualism to Descartes, I think the human fall into dualism is described long before Descartes, in the third chapter of Genesis.

Whereas Adam and Eve were created whole, one with their own deepest being-in-God's-Being and therefore one with each other and the natural environment, their individual consciousnesses deluded them into thinking that they could do better for themselves in a state of separation from the Creator's Will and Being. (Alas, the Creator's will and Being turned out to be their own deepest will and being!) In this way they fell out of harmony with their own inner being, with the cosmic process, with each other, and with the environment. And thus began history as we know it—one long story of *either/or*, fragmented, alienated thinking, which exploits other people and dominates and devastates the natural environment. But God, yearning to bring us back to an acceptance of the wholeness in which we were created, seeks to create in Christ's Body *one new person instead of two*.

The "twoness" of Jewish and gentile converts that threatened to split the early church was both a symptom of the old nature, which God wants to transcend in the New Creation, and a manifestation of the dualistic *either/or* thinking that has always plagued humankind. During the past few years I have been trying to transcend, in my own thinking, various dualisms to which I had become so accustomed that they seemed to be eternal verities: evangelism versus social activism; death versus life; profane versus sacred; body versus mind; means versus end; the many versus the one; the particular versus the general; the relative versus the absolute; good versus evil; matter versus spirit; human versus divine. Not only does human nature tend to split reality in terms of such opposites, but we then arrange everything in hierarchies, assuming that, of course, life is better than death, mind is better than body, the divine is better than the human, and so forth.

Small wonder, then, that we have gone on from there and have arranged the creatures we see around us in a hierarchy of value. Those people in power have consistently defined the norm in terms of themselves and have assumed the superiority of those within the power group over those outside the power group. Thus, males have defined themselves as centrally and normatively human, with females as the naturally inferior other. We whites have defined ourselves as the norm, with people of all other colors as the naturally inferior others. We citizens of the United States have defined ourselves as the norm, reserving the name Americans for ourselves, as if Latin Americans, Central Americans, American Indians, and Canadians did not have just as much right to the name as we do; and naming ourselves Americans has made us feel free to step on the others, who do not feel quite as important to us as we feel to ourselves. We Westerners have looked down on Orientals, so that without embarrassment we could read and recite Tennyson's "Better fifty years of Europe than a cycle of Cathay." We who have comfortable incomes have looked down on the poor, sniffing that if they had only worked as hard as we have, they would not be poor. And of course the heterosexual majority defines itself as the norm, naturally superior, and knows what names to call the homosexual minority, who will be granted provisonal acceptance if they will accept the majority's definition of them as either sinful or sick. The list of dualisms and hierarchies could go on indefinitely.

But it seems to me that God is trying to make oneness out of the twoness that has divided us against ourselves and against one another. When I take a good hard look at the Structure-and-Process of Reality (at the Way Things Are) I discover that my dichotomies operate in a dialectical fashion so closely related to each other that the one *becomes* the other, and airtight separations are only apparent or artificial. For instance, when Joseph confronted the brothers who had sold him into slavery, he said something that collapses the positive versus negative categories I think I am so expert at recognizing: "You meant evil against me," Joseph said, "but God meant it for good" (Gen. 50:20). And Jesus remarked that what the human ego thinks is life is frequently death and vice versa, and even that the experience of life is simultaneous with the experience of death: "Unless a grain of wheat falls into the earth and dies, it remains alone; but if it dies, it bears much fruit" (John 12:24). Thus, the experience of being born into the New Creation is simultaneously death to the old nature.

Only recently have I become sensitized to the dualistic overtones of racist phrases that associate blackness with evil, such as *blacklisting,* and *blackballing,* and *black moods,* and *black magic.* Not only do these dualisms hurt other people; they also hurt me by blunting my imagination so that I am less likely to be able to see God in the other. It is interesting that when the children of Israel were wandering in the desert, God appeared to them always in the other. When it was bright day, God led them through a dark pillar of cloud or smoke. When it was dark night, God was present in the pillar of bright fire. (Milton captures this fact in a paradox, speaking of God's robes as "dark with excessive bright.") To view "the other" as inferior is to cut myself off from the awareness of God's presence.

As we believers face the future, I think we are being challenged to forego our *either/or* thinking in favor of a *both/and* mentality. Instead of the mentality that assumes that somebody has to lose so that somebody else can win, I think we are being asked to see that if we worked at it, we could discover a way in which everybody could win. Certainly those of us who have experienced successful long-term friendships or have known success in marriage have learned that in a close interpersonal relationship, either *both* people win or *both* people lose. As the old adage puts it, "Win an argument, lose a friend." Although many traditionalists have tried to tell us that the male is to be dominant in a Christian marriage, the fact is that Jesus spent his whole teaching career trying to get across to his disciples that dominance/submission relationships follow a worldly model and that mutuality and cooperative servanthood are the Christian model. Within that model, both persons win.

Ironically, it has taken the Women's Movement to bring mutuality to the attention of the world in the twentieth century. The Christian churches should have been standing over against the patriarchal culture for centuries, preaching and modeling mutual submission, concern, and servanthood. Instead, Christian institutions have been modeling themselves after the worldly dominance and submission concept and have formed some of the biggest hierarchies of them all. Even today, when women are trying to have our equal rights guaranteed by a constitutional amendment, many Christian church people are in the forefront of opposition to the ERA. And many Christian business organizations currently hide under a privileged private status that makes them exempt from having to obey government dictates on affirmative action. Thus we have the spectacle of supposedly Christian organizations that, in their personnel practices, are more racist and more sexist than many secular organizations.

For about a decade the Women's Movement has been challenging the hierarchical model of our society, calling instead for a more fluid arrangement of power. Instead of assuming that power is properly a matter of birth categories, such as race, sex, nationality, or class, feminists are calling for a recognition of the dignity of all human beings. In particular, Christian feminists are arguing that authority and leadership in church and home should go to those persons who have the requisite spiritual gifts and have developed those gifts responsibly. Since the New

Testament tells us that the Holy Spirit distributes gifts without regard for race, sex, age, or economic status (Acts 2; I Cor. 12; Rom. 12), we feminists have the force of Scripture behind us. On the other hand, we must be constantly vigilant to guard against assuming that because we are working for sexual justice, our cause is the ultimate cause and more important than any other cause. To make that assumption is to fall into the same old *either/or* ego-trap of building hierarchies based on *Us* versus *Them*.

One of the dualisms that seems to strangulate the imagination of many church people is the dualism between clergy and laity. (This one hasn't been such a problem for me, since there was no formal ordination in the Plymouth Brethren Assemblies.) I think healthy developments might be encouraged in the church of the future by learning from the activities of the Latin American "base communities," those small groups of Catholics who meet together, without benefit of clergy, to study the Bible, to worship, and to carry their theological reflections into action. The thriving nature of these Christian cell groups presents a powerful alternative to our current concept of the church as a hierarchical institution. I am reminded of the early church, when Christians apparently met frequently in homes, such as that of Priscilla and Aquila (Rom. 16:5), "breaking bread from house to house" (Acts 2:46), and providing a great deal of communal support for one another, including voluntary communism (Acts 4:32-35). Similar carrying of our faith into the community and into daily involvement should break down the secular/sacred dualism as well as the worst aspects of the clergy/laity dualism. In the process, perhaps all of us will more fully act out the injunction of I Corinthians 10:31: "So, whether you eat or drink, or whatever you do, do all to the glory of God."

12
Ego-Reduction as a Faith Agenda

As I think about the church, Christ's Body, in the 1980s and thereafter, what I keep wondering is, "How shall we go about being God's servants in a world where the cries of distress continue to sound? By what agenda can we move together toward the 'previous future' of mutuality, global justice, and peace under the reign of the Christ-nature? How does the mystical reality get converted into a practical reality?"

Inevitably, my thinking is limited by my own angle of perception. But of this I feel sure: the broad underlying principle of hope is that of reducing the ego-element, reducing the body-identified myopia that causes hostility and erects barriers between God's creatures. As I never cease marveling over, it is in the womb of God that all of us live, move, and have our being (Acts 17:28), and Christ shared human nature so that we human beings might share the divine nature (II Pet. 1:4). When John the Baptist said concerning Jesus, "He must increase, but I must decrease" (John 3:30), he was giving to all of us the paradigm for the faith journey in our era and every era: that our private ego-gratifications must diminish to make room and ever-*greater* room for Christ's mind, for the viewpoint-of-the-whole, for the divine nature, to live in us. Therefore it seems to me important to think about some of the practical implications of this "dying into life."

For one thing, I think that for United States citizens, ego-reduction will mean learning to share our resources in a shrinking world economy. This belief was especially impressed upon me by a book called *The Emerging Order*, written by political activist Jeremy Rifkin (G. P. Putman, 1979). Rifkin describes with approval the biblical position that "sin is people's hubris in believing that they can treat God's creations differently than God does—namely, manipulate and exploit them for purposes other than what they were created for. . . . A Christian must love God's creation and treat it with respect because God created it with love." Rifkin points out that for the past five hundred years, Reformation theology as refined by the Enlightenment and the Liberal Ethos has provided a thelogical undergirding for an economic era of constant expansion. Now, however, because we are running out of energy sources, the Age of Growth is at an end. And another Reformation theology is beginning to surface to match the economic situation. Radical evangelical scholars, says Rifkin, are striking down the assumptions of the expansionary epoch by teaching "dominion as stewardship rather than ownership, and conservation rather than exploitation."

Although human beings cannot hope to restore the world to its original perfection before the fall (since only

God can perfect the New Earth), Rifkin points out that human beings are currently faced with a major decision. Will we align ourselves with those who speed up the entropy process by continued and accelerated consumption, using up the world's resources without concern for those who are now starving and those who will come after us? Or will we align ourselves with those who are attempting to preserve God's creation and thus to slow down entropy and "extend the life of the world's ecosystem"? It seems to me that the second position is the only one possible for biblical people.

If I am correct about that, then ego-reduction will necessitate the simplifying of life-styles, even though the "simplifying" may sometimes be more expensive in money or personal effort. Some will learn to heat our homes with replaceable resources, such as wood, or by harnessing solar or wind energy. Some will acquaint ourselves with the physical and spiritual virtues of fasting. Some will pool resources in communal living. There is no reason why residents of the United States should continue to consume more than a third of the world's resources. Mutuality demands that our global concern increase while our national egotism shrinks.

I hope that a major part of ego-reduction for people of faith will be active opposition to the insanity of the nuclear arms race. By the beginning of the 1970s, there already was enough stockpiled nuclear weaponry to equal fifteen tons of dynamite for every person on earth. How much overkill do we need? As R. D. Laing has commented, "We are them to them as they are them to us." If we persist in our mad delusion that we can protect ourselves from Them with weapons that will destroy Us in the bargain, all of us will self-destruct together in one huge sacrifice on the altar of the ego. Despite technological advances, what has always been true remains true: genuine safety comes not by might, not by the power of military machinery, but by God's Spirit (Zech. 4:6).

I think that especially wise restraint and balance will be required of United States citizens as our domestic affairs adjust to the loss of the "expansion frontier." The fewer goodies available, the more various citizens are pitted against one another. Because jobs are scarce, for instance, women and racial minorities are frequently pitted not only against white males but against each other, with devastating internal results for those who are both women and racial minority members. And of course "last hired, first fired" policies are militating heavily against racial minorities and women, who generally were the last hired. Many a priest or minister who knows that it is unjust to block women's rise to full equality in the pulpit and church government may be tempted to repress that vision in the face of shrinking job opportunities. Many feminists may lose their vision of racial justice, and vice versa, in the face of shrinking job opportunities. I cannot specify what decisions ego-reduction will lead to in individual cases; I can only constantly remind myself that it is sub-Christian to place "me and mine" before balanced concern for all members of God's creation.

Jeremy Rifkin points out that charismatic Christians with their faith-healing and tongues are currently providing an important challenge to the idolatry of science and technology, which has been so rampant during the era of economic expansion. But he also warns that many people in the charismatic and evangelical movements are beginning to fall back on the old ploy of the "Gospel of Wealth," equating biblical doctrine with "rugged individualism, free enterprise, and unlimited material accumulation." If it were made an "adjunct to right wing and capitalist policies," Rifkin warns, Christian doctrine could "provide the necessary self-imposed order that a fascist movement in America would require to maintain control over the country during an era of long-range economic decline." I have an urgent sense that Rifkin is right. Unless middle-class Christianity learns that the *central* sign of the Holy Spirit's anointing is the bringing forth of justice on the earth (Isa. 42:1-4; Luke 4:18-19), we are liable to see the Christian renewal movement become a pawn in the hands of a neo-fascist regime. We who care had better speak out, without delay, on the subject of universal, covenant concern for justice to those we have formerly classified as secondary to ourselves.

In the area of missions (sharing the good news with others), I believe ego-reduction points toward *contextualization* as opposed to mere *indigenization*. Whereas the indigenous mission agenda focused on cultural factors like finding relevant signs and symbols and appropriate forms of organization, contextualization goes a step further and seeks to place the gospel witness in an *all-inclusively* human context. Not just culture in the narrow sense, but also social, economic, and political factors are taken into consideration. For women, nonwhites, homosexuals, and the poor, this means that a gospel that perpetuates their secondary status is *not* Good News at all and therefore is *not the gospel*.

Charles Taber, who developed the concept of contextualization, defines it this way: "Contextualization . . . is the effort to understand and take seriously the specific context of each human group and person on its own terms and in all its   dimensions—cultural, religious, social, political, economic—and to discern what the

Gospel says to people in that context. . . . It does not, for instance, ask how the Gospel relates to 'the religions,' but how it relates to *this* religion as understood by *this* group or *this* person. [It asks] what genuine insights does this [people's religion] offer into the character, activity, and will of God? What are its gaps, its errors, its distortions? . . . It is on the basis of such an analysis," Taber concludes, "that contextualization tries to discover in the Scriptures what God is saying to these people." (For further information about contextualization, write to Partnership in Mission, 1564 Edge Hill Road, Abington, Pennsylvania 19001.)

Several assumptions in Taber's statement seem to me particularly important for the immediate future among people of faith. First, Taber's definition of the gospel assumes concern for the whole human situation; nothing less will do. Second, there is an ego-reducing sense of openness and mutuality with the people to whom we bear witness—a sense of being changed and helped by those we seek to change and help. This means, as Taber points out elsewhere, getting over the *positivistic fallacy* of identifying truth solely with verifiable facts and scientific precision. It also means getting over the *materialistic fallacy* that the person or organization that puts up the money has the right and responsibility to call the shots.

Mission boards, Taber suggests, need to approach their national churches with a statement of repentance for instituting programs without adequate consultation with the people involved, with a request for a complete overhaul under the initiative of the nationals themselves, and with a promise to relinquish the control which has been giving the nationals the message that their hard work is less valuable than the mission board's money. As foreign as all this is to the concept of missions I have heard all my life, I am convinced that Taber is right. Precisely this kind of mutuality and respect is a *primary need* in any person or group that has been oppressed along racial, class, or sexual lines.

Third, Taber assumes that the discipline of listening to other people's definitions of their own needs, beliefs, and agenda must then send us back to the Bible to discover its message for those people with their specific needs, beliefs, and priorities. Obviously, I am in profound agreement with that biblical emphasis and with Taber's sensitivity to the necessity for constant dialogue between timeless Scripture and timely context. Too much focus on timely context will bring about rootless trendiness. Too much focus on timeless Scripture without twentieth-century context will bring about rigid, self-righteous irrelevance. Balance, O God, grant us balance!

Finally, I am convinced that ego-reduction does *not* mean that I must deny or wipe out my own individuality. Paradoxically, the more I die to my false self with its superficial ego-gratifications, the more my energy is freed up to be fully individuated, so that I become more thoroughly and happily myself. No longer do I have to pretend nervously that I am blind to skin color. Because I know that every race and nation is united in Christ, I can own and enjoy the fact that I am a white person who has certain gifts to contribute to the mutual interaction between people of various colors. Because of oneness in Christ, I can own and enjoy the fact that I am a woman, interacting in mutuality with my brothers and sisters everywhere. I can admit and enjoy my personal power and the gifts God has given me, because I know that the use of that power and those gifts in the service of others will enrich both them and me. I can also "relax" into community, confident that where I am weak, someone else will have gifts of strength, which will enrich us all. And my grateful acceptance of help will strengthen not only me, but also my helper! In short, the more I die to the ego's assumption that others are secondary to me, the more fully I will be able to enjoy the freedom of the Christ-nature. I am never less myself than when seeing only myself; never more myself than when seeing my interrelationship with the All-in-all!

13

The Divine Worth of Gay Persons

In June 1979, the General Synod of the Reformed Church of America voted to ordain women after many years of debate. Having been part of their debate by speaking at Western Seminary and publishing a lengthy article in the *Reformed Journal*, I was astounded to discover on what basis the matter was finally resolved. According to the news report I saw, the resolution hinged on the meaning of the word "persons" in the denomination's Book of Church Order. Traditionally, "persons" had been interpreted as designating males only. Apparently, not until 1979 was the category of "personhood" opened up to include females as well! Anybody who needs additional proof that the language issue is not a trivial one ought to ponder that development for a while!

Perhaps because of having endured such massive

assaults on our human dignity, church women seem able more readily than men to resonate with the pain of gay persons in a homophobic society. In 1973 I met Letha Scanzoni at a conference on women held at the Conservative Baptist Theological Seminary in Denver. With Nancy Hardesty, Letha had already co-authored the ground-breaking book on evangelical feminism, entitled *All We're Meant to Be* (Word, 1974). Partly as a result of Letha's staunchly supportive friendship and the warm friendship of her husband, sociologist John Scanzoni, I was empowered to write my own contribution to Christian feminism, *Women, Men, & the Bible*. And in 1978 Letha and I further developed our mutual concern for biblical ethics and social justice by writing a book together: *Is the Homosexual My Neighbor? Another Christian View* (Harper & Row, 1978).

It was one of seventeen books published in a single season which claimed to examine homosexuality from a Christian perspective. And ours was the only one of the seventeen to advocate that homosexual relationships be evaluated on the basis of *quality of relating* rather than the "object" with whom the relating is done.

To say that all sexual relating between persons of the same sex is always and unequivocally wrong is to undercut, indeed to deny, the personal worth of homosexuals. Constitutional homosexual orientation is a *state of being*, established by about age five, in which the individual's most authentic and therefore deepest and holiest love-feelings flow naturally toward persons of the same rather than the other sex. To treat these love-feelings on a par with gang rape, adultery, prostitution, and acts of flagrant exploitation is to defame and deny homosexual personhood. Some homosexual unions (covenant relationships) have been loving, supportive, and "monogamous" for twenty or thirty years or more—despite all the societal pressures aimed at breaking up such relationships. Yet many church leaders persist in comparing such unions to sicknesses like alcoholism, or violations of covenant like adultery, or exploitation like bestiality. Such insensitivity fills me with rage and pain on behalf of the people whose highest love nature is being treated with contempt.

Fortunately, the publication of *Is the Homosexual My Neighbor?* has opened up opportunities for me to speak to a variety of gay audiences. I have been delighted to share with those audiences my convictions about the unconditional love of God, the divine worth of *every* human being, and the importance of transcending societal damage by retraining the unconscious mind to accept one's sexual nature as a good gift of God and then learning to use the gift responsibly.

By saying that every homosexual act is intrinsically evil, the church has unwittingly encouraged irresponsible behavior among gay persons. (Told that whatever they may choose to do to express their authentic natures is always by definition going to be evil, is it so unusual for people to despair, grow defiant, and act devil-may-care?) The amazing factor is that so many gay Christians have managed to live responsible and meaningful lives despite the abuse heaped upon them.

Why have so many church people been so cruelly insensitive toward gay personhood? The answer is very complex; I will focus on just two components that seem to me of great importance.

First, a great many people seem enraged that many homosexual persons refuse to accept society's verdict that they are either sinful or sick. For instance, a Yale theology professor in July of 1979 claimed that medical and theological doctors still have not found out whether homosexual acts are "expressions of love or symptoms of self-hatred and the aggressive need to humiliate others." Thus Professor Muehl continues to treat homosexuals not as *persons* but as a *category*. (After all, just like "heterosexual acts," "homosexual acts" could be *any* of the above, depending on the individuals and their situations.) Muehl sweeps aside all the authoritative scientific studies cited in the book Letha and I wrote, as well as other more recent studies which find that when examined with proper scientific objectivity, the homosexual orientation appears neither sinful nor sick and therefore that homosexual persons are as capable as anybody else of loving, supportive relationships. Until recent years, the homosexual orientation was described on the basis of samples taken either from prison or from psychiatric case studies. (How would the heterosexual orientation look, I wonder, if described only through studies of prison inmates and people in psychiatric wards?) If people were careful to cite only fully documented, carefully validated studies based not on a few random samples but on adequate samplings, it would not be possible to make depersonalizing claims like Professor Muehl's.

Second, a great many people still assume that the Bible repudiates homosexuality. But the fact is that the Bible never mentions the homosexual *orientation*, which was unknown until the beginning of the twentieth century. And the Bible never mentions homosexual *love*, either— only certain same-sex *abuses*, such as attempted gang rape (Gen. 19), lust as an expression of idolatry (Rom. 1), and what seems to be exploitative and extortionistic homosexual prostitution (I Cor. 6:9; I Tim. 1:10). Since the Bible is silent about both the homosexual *orientation* and homosexual *love*, that leaves concerned Christians free to formulate our attitudes and policies through careful study of scientific research and through honest, open dialogue between the gay and heterosexual communities.

Some Christians have argued that the Genesis creation accounts make it impossible for them to accept modern scientific findings that the homosexual orientation is neither sin nor sickness but simply a minority orientation, an anomaly. "God created Adam and Eve," the argument goes, "not Adam and Bruce or Eve and Helen. Therefore God's exclusive channel for approved sexual relating is heterosexual marriage." Among the many problems introduced by this argument are two major literary problems. First, the argument ignores the poetic, mythic quality of the Genesis language, placing upon it a scientific burden the language was never intended to bear. Second, the argument ignores the fact that Genesis 1 and 2 are creation narratives, descriptions of how the human race was spawned; so by definition the relating had to be heterosexual, fertile coitus. If the Genesis accounts are taken to exclude homosexual union, they must also be taken to exclude any heterosexual acts other than coitus (penis in the vagina), any attempt at birth control, and singleness for any reason whatsoever.

A contextual reading of the creation narratives sees them as mandating the co-humanity of males and females, a co-humanity that may be expressed in convenantal relationships (marriage) and also by working harmoniously with the other sex in church and society. In my visits to gay activist and gay church groups I have seen many examples of co-humanity in action: beautiful equal-partner cooperation between males and females. Anything which breaks that co-humanity, such as the centuries-old assumption of male primacy or the recent separatist position that women should repudiate all cooperation with men, seems to me a violation of biblical co-humanity. But gay covenantal relationships do not violate co-humanity, because they do not rule out—rather, they provide support for—loving and harmonious interaction with the other sex in church and society.

My own faith-journey of the past decade convinces me that the church community is seriously *harming itself* by its dehumanizing attitudes toward gay men and lesbians, and in particular by its refusal of first-class citizenship in the church. I believe it is time for all twentieth-century Christians to remind ourselves that the sharpest point of controversy in the early church was whether converts from paganism, the Gentiles, should be forced to become Judaized by being circumcised and following other Jewish purification rites and ceremonies. For a conscientious Jewish person, brought up in careful observance of the law and then converted to faith in Christ Jesus, it seemed nothing less than scandalous to allow Gentiles to achieve full acceptance in the church without the observance of Jewish customs. Jewish converts could cite passage after passage in their Bible, the Old Testament, to prove that people who did not observe Jewish law and ritual could not possibly be the children of God's promise to Abraham. We learn from the fifteenth chapter of Acts that their perfectly honest scruples were overcome in two ways: first, through repeated reminders that everybody gets salvation the same way, through faith in Christ Jesus; and second, through the apostolic accounts of how the Holy Spirit was working in the gentile converts.

I believe that the contemporary rejection of gay

Christians can be overcome in similar fashion. Instead of requiring that gay people try to *earn their salvation* by giving up responsible expression of their sexuality, the Christian church needs to remind itself that everybody gets salvation the same way, not through works but through *grace*. And the church needs to pay attention to the remarkable work the Holy Spirit has been doing through homosexual Christians. Ephesians 3:6 makes the statement that "the Gentiles are fellow heirs, members of the same body, and partakers of the promise in Christ Jesus through the gospel." For many conscientious Jewish converts to Christianity, that statement was as mind-blowing as if Ephesians had been written today and had addressed heterosexual Christians with this message: "Homosexual Christians are fellow-heirs, members of the same body, and partakers of the promise in Christ Jesus through the gospel." By analogy, that *is* one of the messages the book of Ephesians gives to the contemporary church—and the message can be ignored only to the detriment of the entire Body of Christ.

Unless church communities open their arms to gay Christians and preach the good news of God's unconditional love to people of all persuasions, they will continue to place themselves under judgment (Rom. 2:1) and cut themselves off from their own heritage of being rooted and grounded in Christ's love (Eph. 3:17-19). What we give is what we get. Sow judgmentalism, reap the feeling of being under judgment. Sow acceptance of others, reap self-acceptance. Sow the love of God, reap the sense of being loved by God. It is high time for the heterosexual majority to be *kinder to itself* by accepting and affirming the divine worth of *all* persons.

14
The Inevitable Unity of Liberation Movements

Valerie Russell, mentioning the fact that the same seeds which spawn the white racist mentality also spawn the sexist mentality, correctly explained that we who seek to combat sexism and white racism "are not asking for a bigger piece of the American pie, rather we are seeking to formulate a new world." It is imperative, I think, that church leaders recognize that Christian feminists are not trifling, not simply ego-centered, but increasingly global of vision and utterly serious. We want male leaders to move over and make room for us at all levels of decision-making and leadership—not because we believe in hierarchy, but because until we have power we cannot use power to empower those who have no power. When all of our church institutions have women and minority clergy and decision-makers at all levels of power *in proportion to their numbers in the pews,* that will be the day that we will know the religious system is no longer sexist and racist.

I hope that church leaders in the 1980s will bring the biblical vision of human equality through mutual submission to the attention of church people so insistently that the vision will actually be implemented. I have already admitted that "in honor preferring one another" will be a very hard saying in a shrinking economy. It may sometimes mean voting a reduction in one's own salary in order to retain the service of some last-hired minority men and women; it may even mean stepping down from a highly lucrative or honorable post in favor of a nonwhite or a woman. Equitable distribution is nevertheless the "bottom line" of mutuality.

We women are tired of being trivialized. As Carter Heyward and Suzanne Hiatt pointed out, the stand taken by the U.S. Episcopal bishops that no Episcopalian will in any way be penalized for refusing to accept women priests "springs from a deeply held, though seldom articulated, view of liberals and conservatives alike—that matters concerning women are really not very important, certainly not worth breaking up the old gang over. The 'rights and wrongs' involved in such questions as the ordination of women always take a back seat to 'more important things,' such as world hunger, disarmament or war. Interestingly enough, such questions as the ordination of women—something the church could do something about—are set aside most often to debate matters the church is at present unable to affect seriously one way or another" (*Christianity and Crisis,* June 26, 1978). I pray that church renewal will become more truly biblical by changing this pattern in the near future.

I also hope that people working in various liberation movements, and those working primarily in resistance to ungodly tendencies in first-world government, will perceive the profound unity of all such movements and will support one another rather than acting like jealous rivals. Let me illustrate the deep-seated identity of various liberation and resistance concerns by mentioning some parallels between feminist and black theology.

First, James H. Cone says that he rejects Marxism because it reduces every contradiction to class analysis and thus ignores racism as a legitimate point of departure in the liberation process. He says, "I will not listen to anybody who refuses to take racism seriously, especially when they themselves have not been victims of it." In the light of what I've just said about the continual shunting aside of women's concerns, the parallel should be obvious. We biblical feminists must be prepared to take the same stand. Mutuality teaches us to listen to others and seek to empower others, and that is what we have been doing. But we cannot continue to serve those perspectives which continually refuse to take sexism seriously. Mutuality is by definition two-directional. Cone says, "If we [blacks] are to be free, we black people will have to do it" (*Cross Currents,* Summer 1977). And if we women are to be empowered, we feminists will have to do it. Our concern is global, and we yearn to lend asistance to liberation and resistance to injustice everywhere—but we look not for one-directional serving, which becomes servility, but rather for genuine mutuality among the various movements. We welcome the assistance of *male* feminists as an expression of the oneness of Christ's Body, and we seek and expect reciprocity from the various movements to which we lend our energies. Like black theologians, feminist theologians will have to come to the point that we do not listen to anybody who refuses to take sexism seriously.

Second, in 1977 the National Conference of the Black Theology Project sent out a message to the black church and community that greeted everyone in the name of Jesus Christ, "the Black Messiah and Liberator." The message went on to explain that "the blackness of Jesus is a religious symbol of oppression and deliverance from oppression." The parallel in feminism is of course, the realization of the feminine component in the Godhead. As I described earlier, feminism freed me from the enslaving anthropomorphism of worshiping a God made in the male image. And out of that same liberation, I have gone on to peel away the delusion of worshiping a God made in the *white* image.

I remember, during my college years at Bob Jones University, doing child evangelism in the shanties and shacks of Greenville, South Carolina. We taught the Wordless Book to little black children, showing them that although their hearts were black with sin (black page), if they would trust in Jesus' blood (red page), he would make their hearts white (white page), and take them to heaven (gold page). I deeply repent of the racism and economic heresy I helped propagate in my ignorance at that time. But the memory of it drives home to me the fact that feminist theology with its emphasis on the "femaleness" of God and black theology with its Black Messiah are doing enormously liberating things for human thinking and speaking about God. Instead of groaning about the difficulties of making our liturgical language more inclusive, we ought to be rejoicing in the expansion of our image of God.

Another excellent service performed by both black theology and feminist theology—and by ethnic theologies generally—is to emphasize the physical as well as the spiritual nature of human beings. As the Black Theology

Project put it, "Ultimate salvation and historical liberation are inseparable aspects of the indivisible gospel of
Jesus." Because females have been associated with the
body while males have been associated with the mind,
sexist society has given disproportionate emphasis to
cognitive matters in both schools and churches. The
result has been the dry-as-dust doctrinal emphasis of
white churches and the loss of global sympathy and
values-perception in United States education. Churches
and schools in the 1980s can only *profit* from black
theology's "Soul" and practicality, and from the nurturant, concrete emphases of biblical feminism. Ethnic
and feminist theologies form one chorus of insistence
that the church must emerge from its stained-glass
security and dwell where mothers and fathers are jobless
and crying and where children are hungry.

Fourth, the National Office for Black Catholics
declared in 1974 that "if the Church's reflection on
'Evangelization in the Modern World' is to be productive
in the black community, then it must consider as real that
community's awareness of itself, its [own] assessment of
its needs, and its [own] statement of its aspirations." This
need for self-definition and autonomy is just as urgent
for women and gay people as it is for ethnic groups.

The fifth and final parallel I will mention is the fact
that both blacks and women have been defamed by the
traditional symbols of a white racist culture, symbols
which elevate day, light, the sun (all traditionally
masculine) over night, darkness, and the moon (all
traditionally feminine). Dorothee Sölle makes the point
powerfully in *Death by Bread Alone* (Fortress Press, 1978):
"Our culture denies the 'values of the night' and goes to
excess in illuminating everything. . . . But everything
that grows and lives also needs darkness. Children look

for a cave, a little corner in which to hide; adults build a church that represents darkness and warmth. . . . The Christian Romantic Poet Clemens Bentano illustrates this need for darkness in the lines

> O mother, please keep your
> Little child safe and warm;
> The world's so cold and bright."

I am sustained by the faith that there is hope for individuals, the church, and the world of the 1980s if we will move beyond *either/or* dichotomies and toward mutuality, being "subject to one another out of reverence for Christ" (Eph. 5:21). Partnership between humanity and God's "Allness" can create a breadth of thought and action that leaves room for darkness as well as light, female and ethnic experience as well as male and white experience. In short, getting beyond hierarchical idolatries can open our eyes to the rejuvenating fact that everyone who lives is of divine worth, and indeed that everything that lives is holy. Since it is by the sustaining energy of Christ that everything *does* live (Col. 1:17), such perception is an act of worship. There is no bush that does not burn. There is no ground that is not holy ground.

As part of the speech segment of my life, I have become aware of the interior journey of many literary giants. Now, during my daily periods of silence, I often find myself praying the words which one of them, Percy Bysshe Shelley, addressed to the West Wind, symbolizing the divine Spirit: "Be thou me, impetuous one!" *Not I but Christ living in me.* Out of speech and silence, I sense what my next action should be; and then there is nothing left except to *do it,* in God's name, and so I will. **I do.**